Praise for *Escaping into the Open*

"If you've always wanted to write, but were afraid to get started, Berg will have you at your desk, pen in hand, soon after you finish your first chapter." —*The Reader's Edge*

"That is a really good book about how to write." —*Booklist*

"Elizabeth Berg's writing exercises are wonderfully inventive. They capture the play and pleasures of writing. Her book is an insightful guide that will help both beginning and experienced writers tap into the world of the heart and imagination—places where all stories are born."

—Ronna Wineberg Blaser, president,
board of directors, Tennessee Writers Alliance

"Elizabeth Berg has shown herself to be an author of astonishing talent. What is even more astonishing is the generosity with which she now shares her insights and wisdom of the process of writing. My students have discovered the secret writers within themselves through the use of this joyful tool."

—Mary Mitchell, writing instructor,
Adult Learning Center, Framingham, Massachusetts

"Elizabeth Berg knows how the publishing industry works, how sentences work, and why writers need to answer only to themselves." —C. Michael Curtis, senior editor, *The Atlantic*

"A writer's writing book worth reading." —*Metrowest Daily News*

"A delightfully honest and amusing memoir cum how-to guide. . . . Whatever your goals or aspirations as a writer, this book has something for you. Savor it." —*Virginia Quarterly Review*

ESCAPING INTO THE OPEN

Also by Elizabeth Berg

Novels

Durable Goods
Talk Before Sleep
Range of Motion
The Pull of the Moon
Joy School
What We Keep
Until the Real Thing Comes Along
Open House
Never Change
True to Form
Say When
The Art of Mending
The Year of Pleasures
The Handmaid and the Carpenter
We Are All Welcome Here
Dream When You're Feeling Blue
Home Safe
The Last Time I Saw You
Once Upon a Time, There Was You

Story Collections

Ordinary Life
The Day I Ate Whatever I Wanted

Nonfiction

Family Traditions
Escaping into the Open

ESCAPING
INTO
THE OPEN

The Art of Writing True

Elizabeth Berg

HARPER  PERENNIAL

NEW YORK • LONDON • TORONTO • SYDNEY • NEW DELHI • AUCKLAND

HARPER ● PERENNIAL

A hardcover edition of this book was published by HarperCollins Publishers in 1999.

P.S.™ is a trademark of HarperCollins Publishers.

HarperCollins books may be purchased for educational, business, or sales promotional use. For information, please e-mail the Special Markets Department at SPsales@harpercollins.com.

FIRST HARPER PERENNIAL EDITION PUBLISHED 2012.

Designed by Elina D. Nudelman

The Library of Congress has catalogued the hardcover edition as follows:

Berg, Elizabeth.
  Escaping into the open : the art of writing true / Elizabeth Berg.—1st ed.
      p. cm.
  ISBN 0-06-019179-1
  1. Berg, Elizabeth—Authorship. 2. Women authors, American—20th century—Biography. 3. Fiction—Authorship. 4. Creative writing. I. Title.
  PS3552.E6996Z465   1999
  813'.54—dc21
[B]
                                                                    99-11192

ISBN 978-0-06-220044-0 (Harper Perennial edition)

HB 11.10.2020

*This book is dedicated to Sally Ryder Brady,
gentlest of teachers, wisest of friends.
Also wisest of teachers and gentlest of friends.*

With ongoing gratitude and love.

If thou art a writer, write as if thy time were short, for it is indeed short at the longest.
                                    —HENRY DAVID THOREAU

Contents

Contents

Acknowledgments

Marjorie Braman, then an editor at HarperCollins, was the one who saw the promise in this book when it was just an idea in my head, and she worked alongside me every step of the way as I wrote it. She was and still is a dream to work with: she's smart, perceptive, funny, and charming, and she is my partner-in-crime at the martini bar, though she persists in drinking the wrong kind of gin.

Many years later, it was the ebullient Jennifer Brehl who answered the phone at HarperCollins one day, listened to my request for a new jacket, and not only accommodated that but also helped bring forth this edition, which has some extras that the original edition did not.

I am indebted to the critics who championed this book, to the teachers who use it in their classrooms, and to all the readers who found it inspiring and then took the time to write me letters saying so. I am especially pleased by those readers who wanted to be published and found something in this book that finally made that possible for them. See?

Author's Note

I've been writing professionally for twenty-seven years. I've published hundreds of magazine articles, nineteen novels in eighteen years (many of them *New York Times* bestsellers), two short story collections, and two works of nonfiction. I've always said that, for me, writing is joyful, effortless. But recently the creative road, once so unalterably smooth and sunny, turned dark and bumpy. Doubt crept in, despair. A kind of flat weariness. I needed counsel and inspiration, and one of the places I turned to for help was a book on writing. This is odd, because I'm not really a big fan of books about writing. Even odder is that the book I turned to was my own, the very book you're holding in your hands. And, as immodest as it must sound, I will tell you that I found exactly what I needed. (On page 122, if you must know.)

Escaping into the Open: The Art of Writing True came about because I wanted to have something to refer people to when they asked questions about my "process," even though I agreed with E. B. White who, when he was asked about his process, said he didn't much like to look under the hood. But in writing this book, I did look under my hood, and I offered literally all I know and believe about writing—everything from utilizing your sense of smell to help tell a story to tips for finding an agent. I added my own experiences in the publishing world, and along the way debunked some myths. I put in writing exercises that can be used again and again, as well as some words of great wisdom from other authors, some of whom teach writing. I also included a few recipes, because I like recipes, and my then-editor, Marjorie Braman, was congenial enough to let me do so.

The book was published in 1999, and I went out on tour with it. Book tour is a vulnerable time for a writer; one pays attention to critical reviews, of course, but one *really* pays attention to what the people say, the 99 percent, as it were. At my very first signing, I did my presentation. Afterward, a woman rushed up to be first in line to have her book signed. As I inscribed it, she said, "I have to tell you, I just *loved* this book!"

"Really?" I asked, thrilled.

"Yeah," she said. "That chocolate cake is terrific!" She showed me the page in her book that had the recipe on it (page 218), and it bore the characteristic splatters of a recipe well loved and used.

Happily, she loved more than the recipes. She loved the exercises; she said that through them she discovered something about herself and her mother that she had never known, at least not consciously. Something about the exercises made her dig deep.

All these years after the book was published, I find that it still holds everything I know and believe about writing. People are still buying it. Teachers use it in their classrooms, all the way from elementary school to college and beyond. Writers have told me they keep the book beside them on their desks to function as a silent cheerleader. More than one person has sent me an exuberant letter saying that he or she got something published based on one of exercises in this book. That is why my publisher has reissued it, with a new cover and—bonus!—with a few new exercises, too.

I used to think that books about writing were bogus. I thought they attempted to deconstruct a fragile and dreamy process that by its very nature defied such a thing. I thought that creativity held up under intense scrutiny about as well as love does, and that to try to "capture" whatever makes writing work was the same as capturing a butterfly, which, when it is captured, is no longer a butterfly at all, not really.

But as the great Joni Mitchell says, life is for learning. Writing *Escaping into the Open* taught me that process can be demystified. Technique can be taught. Paying attention, *noticing*, that vital tool that every writer needs to use, can be taught. The need for restraint can be taught, as can the need for expansion with details. And trust can be taught. And retaught, as it seems it must be. When you're a writer, you are a fragile person doing a fragile thing; what must sustain you is your own idea of the worth of your work, even if no one else believes in it—yet.

I still believe that writers are born, not made, that they come into the world with a need to express themselves on paper, whether they seek to be published or not. But I also have come to understand the worth of having a little help now and then, some vital support. *Escaping into the Open* will give you that. As well as a terrific recipe for chocolate cake.

—Elizabeth Berg, 2012

Introduction

> All writing is communication; creative
> writing communication through
> revelation—it is the Self escaping into the
> open.
>
> —E. B. WHITE

I am sitting in a coffeehouse, listening to the big band music they play here, to the explosive sounds of the espresso machines, to the subtler noise of cash registers and conversation. Across from me, a man of about sixty takes the hand of a woman about thirty and looks at her, sighing. Then he starts speaking in a low and urgent tone, in a language I can't understand. Two tables away from me, there is a serious-looking young man with a notebook before him, writing. He was here yesterday, too, doing the same thing. His handwriting is small and cramped, and he keeps one hand over what he's just put down. I'm dying to read it. I want to go up to him and say, "Can I see?" But I won't. Obviously, he's not ready to share. I watch him sipping his coffee, bending over the page to write a few lines, then staring into space, thinking.

It could be that the man is writing a term paper. Or a letter to his father, or to his girlfriend. But I don't think so. There is something about his face, about his manner. I think he's writing something more creative than that, answering an insistent call to transfer what's in him, out.

Last night, as we ate dinner, I told my partner about what I'd done that day. I said I had been to the pet store, where I watched the owner kiss a gray parrot that kissed him right back. I told him about the ragged V shape of the Canadian geese I saw fly across the sky, about the one goose in the rear that honked and honked, complaining about his seat assignment, no doubt. I described the waitress in the restaurant where I ate lunch, a stringy-haired blonde with cigarette breath who talked tough to all her customers, but who made one man finish his orange juice, because he had a cold. And then I told about a taxi driver I'd seen, a man who stood patiently waiting at the cab's open door while his fare walked toward it. She was an old woman, using a walker, and her progress was remarkably slow. But the cab driver did not look at his watch and curse his fate at having a customer who required so much extra care. Instead, he stood smiling, nodding, telling her to take her time, that she was doing just fine. It was a wonderful example of common kindness, the kind of thing that makes you think people are a pretty swell species after all. Everyone who saw that cab driver helping the old woman seemed to experience a certain elevation of spirit, as I did.

My partner listened quietly, as he always does when I tell him all the details of the things I've seen. He knows I have a need to tell stories. But whenever I say them out loud, there is something missing for me. To really tell a story, I need to write it. It's then that I understand what it is that I'm really trying to say. I find the deeper meaning—and the deeper satisfaction.

The same is true of many others. So many people have things they want to say, on paper. Some of these people write freely, and share what they write, even publish what they write.

Others, who have wonderful stories inside them, don't tell them. Or if they tell them, they don't share them. If they don't *want* to share, that's fine. But I believe many people do want to share, do want to write, and are afraid to try. They need a gentle nudge to get going. It is my mission and my high privilege to try to make this book that nudge.

There are people who have never studied writing who are fully capable of being writers. I know this because I am an example. I was a part-time registered nurse, a wife, and a mother when I began publishing. I'd taken no classes, had no experience, no knowledge of the publishing world, no agent, no contacts. What I did have is the same kind of passion I see now in that young man sitting two tables from me. And what I want to say to that young man is what I want to say to anyone who wants to write: You feel the call. That's the most important thing. Now answer it as fully as you can. Take the risk to let all that is in you, out. Escape into the open.

1 *My Story*

Language is the only homeland.
—CZESLAW MILOSZ

The summer when I was nine years old, we lived beside a huge gully. I used to go there nearly every day. Agates and wildflowers were plentiful and free for the taking—you were limited only by the size of your hands and pockets. Near the center of the gully was a secluded embankment covered by blades of grass the length and texture of girls' hair. Willow trees surrounded it, and the sunlight coming through their leaves created a lacy pattern of shadow that I always wished I could pick up and lay over my head like a mantilla. Day after day, I lay on that small hill and watched the shifting patterns of clouds and listened to the birds. I could not identify the birds themselves, but I did recognize their calls. Sometimes I made my own sounds to call back; whenever I did, there would follow a moment of abrupt silence during which I assumed the birds tried to identify me, then gave up and went back to business. I found this satisfying; it made us even.

I could hear the earthbound animals rustling in the grass, sometimes far away, sometimes thrillingly nearby.

The air was warm against my skin, as comfortable as my many-times-washed flannel nightgown. There was the rich smell of black earth everywhere, and I pulled it far down into my lungs, wanting to keep it by making it part of me.

Whenever I was at that place, a sense of peace came into me like a religion. I wanted to tell everyone what it felt like to be there; it seemed like information anyone would want. This happened with many things I saw, or heard, or felt. I wanted to share them. The simplest things mattered so much to me: a school of tadpoles swimming darkly by in the creek behind our house, the thin wail of a baby; the smudged pastels of a sunset; the smell of potatoes frying for Friday night's supper. And the bigger things, too, of course: the mysteries and hurts, the fears and longings, the questions about why and when and how. I had a deep need to give voice to all of these things. I finally started doing it on paper, with poetry.

I wish I could say that I was a precocious child, immediately and highly skilled at the written word. Such was not the case. Here is the evidence, a poem I wrote at nine years old and still remember, so taken with it was I at the time:

Dawn

The sky was dark
The stars shown bright
The city slumbered
In soft moonlight

And out in this beauty
A dog stood alone
Sniffing the air
Sniffing a stone

[I showed this poem to my best friend, Sherry, who said, "Why don't you have the dog sniffing his *bone*?" Well. You can see how readily—and how soon!—editorial interference rears its ugly head. I had to hold on to my sense of aesthetics, of course, to my integrity as a writer and the true owner of my own material. I had to say, "No! I am not going to say 'sniffing his bone'! Then people will think of a greasy, ugly *bone* instead of a beautiful stone!" You can see how vast the difference between the two, I'm sure.]

Anyway, back to the poem. You remember where we were. It's dark, it's late . . .

Out in the alley
A cat licked her paw
Waiting for dawn
And the crow's early caw

A bird made her nest
On into the hours
Weaving among it
Beautiful flowers

Then as dawn
Began to break
Silver sands
Shown by the lake

The elves retired
The people woke
The beauty enchantment
Now was broke

Now, if reading this doesn't give you confidence, I don't know what will. If the person who wrote this now gets to make her living as a writer, think of what you might do!

I am more than a little mortified to tell you that I submitted this poem to *American Girl* magazine, which promptly rejected it, of course. When I got the "no thanks" letter, I lay on my bed and wept. Then I didn't submit anything again for twenty-five years.

This is really true.

However, just because I no longer submitted anything does not mean I stopped writing. I loved writing—themes, essays, letters, everything. I remember once acting up in my junior high science class and being told to write my autobiography as punishment. Some punishment. This was like telling a sugar freak that his "punishment" was to be locked up overnight in a Fanny Farmer store. I turned in my autobiography the next day, and the day after that the teacher handed it back to me, saying stiffly, "This was actually quite good."

"Thank you," I said.

I like to think of this as my first acceptance.

I began to do more creative writing: stories, plays, more poems. I got a lot of encouragement from teachers, from friends—really, from anyone who read what I wrote. My essays were hung up on classroom bulletin boards; a

Christmas poem I wrote was seen by a teacher who asked permission to Xerox it and share it with the faculty. In high school, I was elected president of the Creative Writing Club. This actually was not much of an honor—the club numbered only six; therefore, the position of distinction was that of nonofficer. But never mind. We turned out a literary magazine. I had a poem and a story in it. I was published.

Not that I thought I was a writer. Nor did I have any plans of becoming a writer. I thought writers had to have an education abroad, and wear tweed, and be interestingly tormented. I was only boringly tormented. My plan was to teach English, to have a roomful of students turned on to the written word, courtesy of me. I could write a good essay; I thought I could teach one, too. Then I would get to go to the teachers' lounge, something I was dying to do. I wanted to know what was in the refrigerator they kept in there. I also wanted to sit at the table and smoke with the other teachers, and tell gossipy little stories about students and their parents. I wanted to date the drama teacher, assuming he would be a darkly handsome man, also tormented.

I entered the University of Minnesota as an English major. Alas, I did not like my English classes; I liked my humanities classes. So I switched my major to humanities. And then I didn't want to be a teacher anymore—I wanted to immerse myself in life. It occurred to me that if I wanted to immerse myself in *real* life, I needed to drop out of school.

So I left school and took a job as an information clerk at the Radisson Hotel in downtown Minneapolis, even though I had no information about the hotel or the city at all.

It was an interesting job. I first started drinking coffee there, because the job started very early in the morning and I was always tired when I arrived. So the first thing I used to do was go back into the gigantic hotel kitchen where the friendly cooks were sitting around in their glaring white uniforms drinking their first coffees of the day. They'd give me a cup and insist that I use a saucer, too. Thus armed with caffeine and etiquette, I would proceed to my station.

The man who worked at the front desk with me, the reservations clerk, had a crush on me. He asked if I would like to run away to Majorca with him. "No thank you," I said. And then I asked him where Majorca is. I was more interested in hearing about Majorca than in dispensing information to hotel guests. I didn't like standing behind the front desk in the lobby. I wanted to move around and ask my own questions. I wanted to be behind-the-scenes. I wanted to work with the maids and see what the guests kept in their rooms, and what they left behind. I wanted to hang out in the kitchen with the cooks, listening to their interesting male chatter and watching the reckless way they cooked—those shooting flames coming from those big burners!

I did not stay at that hotel job too long. I was not exactly fired, but I was not exactly encouraged to stay, either. I went on to do many, many other things. I was a receptionist at a law firm; I was a waitress; I washed chickens as a food service worker in a hospital cafeteria. I was the "girl singer" in a rock band, and I acted in an improvisational theater.

Nothing really satisfied me. And then one night I was lying in bed in my terrible cockroach-infested (*not my fault*) apartment in Minneapolis when I heard the person who lived above me throwing up. I mean, throwing *up*. Whoever it was, was really, really sick. I wondered what that person was feeling, what could be wrong with him. I felt an overwhelming urge to go up and help him. I knew exactly what I'd do: straighten his bedclothes, wipe off his face, take him to the bathroom and help him brush his teeth, then put him back into bed and lay a cool washcloth across his forehead. I would say, "Would you like to suck on a lemon? I know it sounds odd, but whenever I'm sick to my stomach, if I suck on a lemon, it helps."

I'm sorry to say I didn't go to offer any help, because the truth is I feared that whoever it was up there would never let me in. The apartment building was . . . well, not the best. One was ill-advised to answer the door in the middle of the night in that building. One could rest assured that it was probably not a delivery of flowers or any other kind of good news at that hour (actually, at any other hour, either). But though I did not help that person, I did decide that helping people was what I wanted to do with my life. Since nuns were required to be celibate, I decided to become a nurse.

I worked as a registered nurse for more than ten years. And I loved it. But even though I worked only part-time after my daughters were born, the hours began to get to me—working holidays, double shifts, every other weekend. I had continued to write, though now it was only letters to friends and in my journals, and people had continued to praise my efforts. My best friend, Phyllis, so believed in my worth as a writer that one year for my birthday she gave me a book of my letters, Xeroxed and bound beautifully in a rich, black volume.

Not long afterward, in 1984, I stopped working as a nurse—I wanted to be at home with my children full-time. I began writing for our small town's newspaper, covering school committee meetings and doing occasional articles on a variety of other topics that ranged from gypsy moths to solar-powered houses. My salary was twenty-five cents per inch of published text.

One day when I had taken my daughter to the library, I came across a copy of *The Writer's Market*. I saw that magazines paid what was to me a small fortune for the articles they bought. I thought, *All right. I'm going to try this.*

I went to the drugstore and bought a bunch of magazines, including *Woman's Day, Family Circle, Good Housekeeping, McCall's, Ladies' Home Journal,* and *Parents*. That month's issue of *Parents* had a notice about an essay contest they were sponsoring—you were to write about some problem in parenting, and how you solved it. The winner would receive five hundred dollars and be published in the magazine. I promptly wrote an essay about the benefits of leaving a job to stay at home with one's children. I also sent a couple of queries out to two other women's magazines.

In a couple of weeks, I got the "no thanks" letters for my queries. In retrospect, I can see why. My query letters were not exactly professional. I had a passion for odd-colored typewriter ribbons, and a need to confess my inexperience right off the bat. (Later we'll get to the *right* way to send out query letters.) I gave up on writing for a living, and went back to being a nurse.

It was almost a year later that I heard from *Parents* magazine. I had moved, and the magazine had not been able to reach me by telephone. Eventually, a letter was forwarded to my new address. I still remember exactly what it felt like when I got that letter. I was standing on the porch in late afternoon sun, rifling through what I'd pulled out of the mailbox. I saw a letter from *Parents* magazine and, thinking it was a solicitation for a subscription I could not afford, I almost threw it away. But the letter looked more personal than that. So I opened it and read: "Congratulations! It's taken us a long time to cull through the thousands of entries we received. . ."

I was to call the magazine so they would know where to send the check. Five hundred dollars! For something I'd written! I couldn't believe it. I thought I'd call and they'd say, "Oh, no, no. Oh, *God* no, *that's* not what we meant!" But they didn't say that. They told me how much they liked the essay, and they asked where to send the money.

When the check arrived, I didn't know what to spend it on. My husband and I had agreed that this check should not be used as the others were—for the electric company, for kids' clothes, for slices of American cheese. This one was to be spent just on me. So the next Saturday, I left my husband with our daughters and went to my favorite store, where I spent all the money on a lot of stuff I neither really wanted nor needed: a purse, scarves, earrings, some art-work. When I got home, I spread everything I'd bought on the dining room table, showed my husband, and then burst into tears. When my husband asked what was wrong, I said, "Look at all this junk! I could have had a KitchenAid *Mix*master instead of all this junk! If I ever sell another article, I'm buying a KitchenAid Mixmaster!"

Well, I did sell another article—to *Parents* magazine, as a matter of fact—and I did buy a KitchenAid Mixmaster, which I still have (and adore—it even grates cheese). I began selling lots of articles to *Parents*, then to other women's magazines.

I was very lucky to have made my first break with *Parents*. My world was tied up with my children at that time, and so they became my material. What's the perfect magazine when your articles are about children? *Parents*, of course. (It remains, by the way, my favorite of parenting magazines, and I would advise anyone writing about children or family to consider them first.) I was also lucky in that the editor of *Parents* at the time was Elizabeth Crow, who was not at all afraid to take a chance on a new writer. She also knew what she liked when she saw it and wasn't afraid to say so. It helped that Elizabeth had children the same ages as mine; that made it easy for her to relate to what I was saying.

Elizabeth Crow was also a writer's dream in that she made her own decisions quickly—she did not pass around manuscripts to a committee of people in order to decide whether or not to buy them. I think her fastest response time was a few days, though it's important to say that this occurred after we'd worked together for a long time—the normal time to wait for a response from a magazine is somewhere between three to eight weeks.

Probably what helped most in starting a career in writing is that the readers of *Parents* were so responsive to my writing style. I am still very grateful to them for giving me the support I needed at that crucial time. Their letters, all of which I still have and occasionally pull out and reread, were essential fuel for the creative fire. They gave me a kind of assurance and comfort; they made me believe I had found the work I really wanted and was meant to do. They legitimized me.

One of the other magazines for which I wrote at the time was the now-defunct *Special Reports* magazine. That magazine branched out into television, and in 1990 I was asked to do videoessays for Special Reports Television. These were three-minute spots in an hour-long program hosted by Joan Lunden, and which aired in doctors' offices. I wrote commentary—sometimes poignant, more often humorous—on family life and women's issues. These were some of the topics: why I carry a big purse, creative cover-ups for fat days, and the differences between the sexes as reflected in semantics. The job necessitated my flying out to San Francisco once a month to film two spots. Tough detail, I know. I stayed at the beautiful Casa Madrona in Sausalito, and I used to eat breakfast looking out at the Bay, thinking, *How can this be true?*

In 1991, I got a call from a book developer named Alison Brown Cerier, who had an idea for a book on family traditions. She had a publisher and a plan; now she needed an author to put it into action. She had called *Parents* magazine looking for the name of a good writer, and I was recommended.

When Alison first called, I was flattered that *Parents* had recommended me. But I was not interested in writing the book she envisioned. First of all, I wanted to write only about what *I* wanted to write about—not because of any stubbornness or ego, but because when other people told me to write about something, I became too concerned with what I thought they wanted to hear. I felt inhibited; it took the joy from writing, and when the joy was gone, anything I attempted was likely to fall flat.

In addition to that, my life was not particularly rich with tradition, not in my growing-up years, and not in my time as an adult. I had *some* traditions in my family, but not enough that I felt qualified to write a book. "Tell you what," Alison said. "Why don't I just send you a proposal so that you can see what it is I have in mind?"

When the proposal arrived, I was a goner. There, in print, on a title page of a book proposal, was my name. I stared at that byline and I thought about how it would feel to have written something that would be preserved between hard covers, something that would have artwork, something that someone could hold in her hands. It was too much to turn down. I felt sure I'd never write another book, certainly not a novel, so this would be a chance for me to have an actual Library of Congress number. I said I'd try a sample chapter. It was kind of fun to do; Alison and her publisher liked the result; and so I agreed to take on the whole project.

What followed were months of what felt like intense homework, because the book required so much research. And though I believed the project was turning out well, that the book would be eminently useful, I often felt resentful writing it. I had no time to work on anything else, including fiction, which I was just beginning to get into. So I made a deal with myself: Every Tuesday, I would allow myself time off from my commitment to Alison to write whatever I felt like writing. I would indulge myself in the dreamy, creative kind of writing I liked best. Thus was born my first novel.

Not that it was meant to be my first novel. I had already started another novel, which is what I'd shown my newly acquired agent, Lisa Bankoff. It was on the basis of that novel that she'd agreed to represent me. I wasn't sure I'd ever really be able to write a novel, but I wanted to try; and I knew that if you wanted to sell a novel, it was important to have an agent. Moreover, my writing life was getting more interesting and more complicated; I felt I needed a partner in making business decisions.

I was sitting at a deli with my agent one morning when I told her that I had a different idea for a novel than the one I'd originally shown her. I gave her two or three pages of a scene describing the way a young girl, who was an Army brat, wasn't allowed to cry when she moved, which Lisa later read standing in line at the post office. She wrote me a note saying that the words sounded very true, as though they were coming from the right place, and that she had really liked reading the pages. That was all I needed to hear.

The nonfiction book was published in November 1992. During the writing of that book, I'd also been working on what became my first published novel. After I had about 120 pages, I sent it to Lisa. In a couple of weeks she called back to tell me she'd read what I'd written thus far. I remember that moment exactly. I'd answered the phone in my bedroom and while we talked, I'd stretched out on the bed. When Lisa said she liked what I'd sent her (her exact words were "Oh, this is just *exquisite!*"), I felt a kind of satisfaction I'd never experienced before.

Lisa sent the partial manuscript to two publishing houses on a Friday. The next Monday morning, both editors who'd received the pages called back saying they wanted to buy the book. The first editor to respond was from Random House. Lisa immediately called me and asked, "How would you like to be a Random House author?" I was literally speechless. Then, while I was on the phone with Lisa, the other editor called, wanting to buy the book, too. Lisa hung up to talk to that editor, and I went out to stand in the living room in my robe, holding the portable phone tightly against my chest and thinking, *This is too much. My life will never have such a moment again.*

Well. That's true, in a way. For me, there was childbirth, and there was that moment of learning that I was going to have a novel published. Despite the wonderful things that have happened to me since (*including* being on *Oprah*), I don't think anything has ever come close to those moments of amazed joy.

I went to New York to meet with the editors, and liked them both. But I decided to go with Random House because of something that editor did. Both editors asked what was going to happen at the end of the book. I couldn't talk about it. I *wanted* to, but I couldn't. It felt as though the lifeblood would be sucked out of the material if I talked about it before I wrote it; it felt like some necessary, vital energy would be gone from me. And so when Kate, the Random House editor, said, "Can you tell me what's going to happen?" I said, "I'm sorry. I just don't think I can talk about it." Kate said quickly, "That's fine." And she meant it. She let me know that she had every confidence that she would like whatever I did. She also let me know that she respected my ways. Many years later, she still does.

After I made my decision, Kate sent me a bouquet with a card saying, "WELCOME TO RANDOM HOUSE." Really, I should have sent *her* a bouquet. Later, my friend Phyllis sent an arrangement of pink roses with a card saying, "THIS IS THE STUFF OF YOUR DREAMS." And so it was.

I've published seven novels now, and I hope to keep producing a novel a year for as long as I can type.

This is what my life is like now:

I live with my dog, Toby, and my cat, Cosette, in a small house in a small town in Massachusetts. My main workplace at home is a converted porch. I have windows on three sides, and I love being able to look out and see trees and birds, grass and flowers (or snow or falling leaves or rain). On my desk are the books I love best: E. B. White's essays and *Black Elk Speaks*. On the bookshelves are other favorites: Alice Munro's and Stephanie Vaughn's stories, novels such as Carson McCullers's *The Member of the Wedding*, novels that friends of mine have written, novels that I have given blurbs to. There is a "magic wand" that lies over the keys of my computer, and taped onto my monitor are a fortune cookie prediction for long life, a Chinese proverb that says "Muddy water let stand will clear," and several quotes. One, from Albert Einstein, says, "Our situation on this earth seems strange. Every one of us appears here involuntarily and uninvited, for a short stay, without knowing why. For me it is enough to wonder at the secrets." Another, from Willa Cather, says, "There was only one thing that had an absolute value for each individual, and it was just that original impulse, that internal heat, that feeling of one's self in one's own breast."

I also work out of a backyard shed, which is plain and simple, stripped down to the basic elements. There is a rag rug, a small desk, a chair before it. There is one very small window. In the corner is an overstuffed chair where I sit when I edit. There are a few books on a cinder-block-and-board bookcase, a few pictures hung on the wooden walls. There is no phone, and it is blessedly quiet.

Oftentimes when I need a break, Toby and I walk to Ed's Place, a tiny restaurant a few blocks from my house, owned by Wayne and Linda Tyler, two of the best people I know. They love and respect their customers, and their customers love and respect them. Toby gets tied to the porch outside Ed's, which is fine with him, because he gets petted and admired by virtually every passer-by; and he usually gets a great treat from Linda, too: left-over bacon, the butt end of a ham, some scraps of buttered toast. I go inside to get two eggs over easy with bacon and hash browns, and I read the newspaper and listen to the great conversations that go on at that place.

Otherwise, I might have coffee and a treat at the bakery, then wander into the hardware store, which I love for its wooden floors and wonderful mix of merchandise—Tootsie

Rolls and sledge hammers, fire starters and packets of flower seeds. Sometimes I go to the post office and buy stamps and shoot the breeze with the interesting and extremely kindhearted people who work there.

When I'm through writing for the day, I return phone calls, clean the house, and cook. On a good day, I'll get a chance to read and work on a quilt, too. If the weather is nice, I try to take Toby to the "doggy playground," a park where many people bring their dogs to let them run free and play with one another.

Sometimes at night, I'll edit what I wrote that day, but most often I'll wait until the next day—I like to read other people before I go to sleep. I keep a mix of novels, essays, poetry, and nonfiction by my bed. These days, I get sent a lot of galleys for blurbs—I keep a fair number of those by my bed, too.

Once a year, I go out on tour for my new books, and, increasingly, I'm being asked to speak and do readings for other occasions. But what I like doing best is writing. Period. Sitting here before the computer and transferring onto the screen the things that I hold in my head and heart. Nothing matches this feeling. Nothing brings me this particular kind of joy. And I need it. I crave it. When I don't have it, I suffer. I feel like a drug addict with an exceptionally wise drug of choice.

There are many glamorous aspects to living the life of a successful writer, but for me the best times are always those that are closest to what I felt when as a child I visited that gully, when I lay on that long, green grass and looked up into the trees and felt the wide ache of wanting to be able to share with someone all that lay inside. To be able to explain things in such a way that another person would say, "Oh. *Yes!*" Through writing, I feel as though I've been able to do that, to connect in some vital way. Never mind the problems I have had in the past or may have in the future; there isn't a day that goes by that I don't know how very lucky I am. Possibly, there isn't an hour.

Homework

Lie down in a quiet place, close your eyes, take some good deep breaths, and clear your mind. Then think about what it is that makes you want to write. What do you remember from your childhood about writing? What form does your writing take now? Would you like a career in writing? If so, in what direction would you like it to go?

Next, fantasize about yourself living the writing life that you want to have. See yourself doing very specific things (Where do you live? What does your writing space look like? What are you writing? Who is reading it? What do they say about it?) and *do not edit yourself in any way,* either by limitation of what you ask for, or by judgment of it. Just have a waking dream about achieving the things you would like to, whether that's writing your memoir for your grand-children or winning a Pulitzer Prize—or both. Remember, the first step in getting what you want is knowing what it is.

2   *Getting Started*

> First, you gotta have heart.
> —RICHARD ADLER AND JERRY ROSS

My daughter knows a man who, upon deciding to go back to school, went to an office supply store to outfit himself with the things he thought he might need. By the time he was through shopping, he was short of the money he needed for tuition. He had to have the best computer, of course. He had to have a lot of ancillary supplies, so he wouldn't have to interrupt his work to run out and buy things. He got a few extra things, too, things that weren't at all necessary but that he thought would be nice to have: a cool trash can, fluorescent-colored Post-its to replace his boring yellow ones, multiple colors of highlighters.

You understand my point in telling you this, I'm sure. When you are first starting to write, you don't need to buy a whole lot of things. What you need most is a fierce desire to put things down on paper; and you need a certain sensibility, a way of seeing and feeling. These things cost nothing and, like many things that are free, are worth a lot—worth everything, in fact.

This morning, I took a walk in the woods to think about

all the other things I believe a writer should have. The good news is that nearly everything I came up with costs nothing. The bad news is that, for some reason, all the things I thought of started with the letter P. Reading an alliterative list can be extremely annoying, I know, but because I am a writer who believes in honoring original instincts, I feel obliged to offer to you exactly what came to me.

Purpose

You need a point, a reason for writing, because this is what will provide the motivation. Perhaps you want to bring an historical figure back to life. Perhaps some extraordinary, life-changing event happened to you or to someone you know, and you want to share it with others. You may feel strongly about the way the world is managed, whether that management is in Washington, D.C., or on Wall Street, or within the confines of a family gathered around the kitchen table; and you may want to spout off about it, offer criticisms and alternatives. Perhaps someone in your family or among your friends has been a true inspiration to you, and you want to thank them—and share them with others—by writing about them. You might have been a natural story-teller since the time you could talk, and now you want to preserve those stories by telling them on paper. You might write in order to teach; or you might write, as I do, in order to learn, to discover things about yourself and others.

Well. I could go on and on, of course. There are literally thousands of reasons someone might have to write. But whatever your reason is, make sure it is truly *your* reason—your passion, in fact. Do not read an article in the newspaper about how books on angels are selling like crazy and think, *Oh, I've got to write a book about angels!!* That is not the kind of passion I'm talking about. Unless, of course, you were passionate about wanting to write about angels before you read the article. Then you can be happy that such books are selling well. (Although knowing the publishing business, by the time your book on angels came out, the hot topic would have switched to devils. You just can't predict *what* will sell well in this business—that's why it's always best to write trying to please an audience of only one—you.)

Plan

If you are going to do more than dream about writing, you need to have a specific plan. You have to decide where, when, and how you are going to get started. The more concrete the details of this plan, the more likely you are to execute it. Deadlines can be a very good thing to impose upon yourself, by the way, when you're setting up such a plan. Take yourself seriously; let yourself be a very high priority. Be willing to invest in yourself financially, emotionally, and spiritually.

Place

Ideally, the place where you write should be an area that is separate from the rest of your house—and life. It should have in it the things you need—tools directly related to the writing craft, say—but it should also be full of the things you love. Once you have created such an area, you really ought to celebrate its birth.

One friend of mine redecorated a home office into a place that was going to be used only for her creative writing. Then she invited all the members of her writing group to come and share in a smudging ceremony. She fed everyone a terrific dinner, then brought the members into the writing room, where she lit candles and filled the air with the scent of burning sage. It meant a lot to my friend to have her writing group there when she initiated her room— she felt as though the space had been blessed twice. Other people are more private, keeping visitors to their workspace to a minimum; and they celebrate the creation of a writing space in the small arenas of their own hearts—and that's good, too.

If at all possible, your writing space should accommodate leaving things set up: It's discouraging to put up and take down your equipment every time you want to work. Richard Bausch says he leaves his computer on all day, then wanders in and out of his study to work on things. That seems ideal to me, the notion of something waiting for you, for whenever you're ready.

Speaking of ideals, what's best is having an entire room in your house or apartment that you can use as a writing space; or, if you have the means, renting an office. But other spaces will do. Consider, for example, using a corner of a bedroom or dining room, or a basement, or a garage, or a shed. Some people take doors off of closets and use that indented area to hold a desk, around which they put a screen.

If there really is no place in your house where you can work, see if you can share office space with someone. A psychiatrist I know rents his office two days a week to a man who's working on a novel. The only problem they've had so far is that the psychiatrist eats the writer's corn chips, but as the psychiatrist is willing to admit to his thievery, the problem is already half solved.

Many cities have writers' rooms, which nurture authors by providing subsidized and therefore low-cost spaces. In Boston, for example, the Writers' Room offers twelve cubicles that can be rented for one hundred dollars a month, or shared for half that. Contact your city's arts council, chamber of commerce, or local branch of the National Writers' Union to determine what is available in your area. Local colleges and universities may also be able to provide such information.

If writers' rooms are not available in your area or if you can't afford to pay rent at all, think creatively about other options: Does a friend have space in her or his house that you might use, in exchange for running errands or babysitting, or for two dozen chocolate chip cookies? How about your local library—can they spare some space where you could stay set up? Is there a nearby school that could help provide you with a quiet, warm, and well-lit place after classes are out for the day? If all else fails, consider using a table at a café or bookstore—it's not always quiet, but it's a separate place that is usually writer-friendly.

When talking about the kind of space that a writer needs, it's important to mention interior space as well. When you write, you need to have a certain willingness inside you; an auto-induced mood of simultaneous quiet and energetic readiness that lets your imagination know it's okay to come out now. It is a kind of respectful laying of the table, in your heart and in your mind, for the guest you want most to come.

You need to work in your space in the way that suits you best. Do you want to write late at night, longhand, on cream-colored paper, under a circle of lamplight, with a glass of wine nearby? Do you want to jump out of bed in the early morning and grab a big mug of coffee and start writing before you've even dressed or brushed your teeth? (Before I got an office, this was how I liked best to write. I would often stay in my pajamas until it was time for the kids to come home from school. The FedEx man always looked at me sympathetically when I answered the door, believing, I suppose, that I was the victim of an incredibly long-lasting virus.)

Also consider things like this: Do you need to take care of all other business and *then* sit down to write, or do you need to write first so that your day is not swallowed whole? Does your desk need to be neat and well organized, or are you more comfortable with a desk that looks like a minor explosion occurred there? Do you want music in the background or do you need absolute silence? Is it good for you to occasionally go to a park and write using a Dixon Ticonderoga No. 2 soft pencil, and a spiral-bound notebook? Or would you like to take a long train ride and sit by the window and write with your beautiful fountain pen in your beautiful journal from Florence?

If you're just starting to write, you may not know the answers to all these questions yet. Be open to finding out about—and accepting—your own particular needs as a writer. Then, if a certain desire comes knocking at your door, let it in. The more you write the way you want to (the way something at your center is telling you to), the better the writing will be.

Perseverance

Don't let rejections of any kind stop you from writing. Period. It doesn't matter what anyone says about anything you do; you can always keep on writing—if not for publication, then for yourself.

But if you are trying to be published, you must be willing to go on in the face of the particular kind of humiliation that rejection brings. We'll talk more about rejection in another chapter, but for now, consider this: One of my magazine articles (one that was among those best received by readers) was rejected seventeen times before it was accepted. It comes to this: If you want to ride, stay on the horse.

Priorities

You've got to be insistent and consistent with yourself and others about making time for writing. This can sometimes be very hard to do. For one thing, people may have a hard time taking seriously your need to write—even if you are many times published.

Also, when you write, you are in charge of your own time; and when you are in charge of your own time, people feel that if you had a decent bone in your body, you would work your schedule around *them*. They don't understand that writing is not like doing laundry, something that can be picked up and put down and returned to at will. They also don't seem to understand that if you are interrupted while you are writing, you can lose thoughts that might never come back.

It can be really bad when people come to visit. If you don't sacrifice your writing time to be with those who have a limited amount of time to spend with you, their eyes can become orphanlike and they can become amazingly creative at finding little ways to make you feel guilty. It's strange. They would understand it if you had an *out*side job you had to go to. But if you're working for yourself, especially if you're working in the house they're staying in, they feel that if you aren't with them, you're slighting them.

Well, listen. You have to be tough. And you can handle it in two ways: You can get dressed before your guests, and as soon as they arise, say, "Oh, good morning! I'm just going out to do a few little errands—I'll be right back. In about six hours." Or you can say, "I'm going to write for a few hours. While I'm working, would you like to [fill in the blank]?" Whatever your approach, once you've figured out the best time of day for your writing, *use that time for writing*. Don't feel you have to continually apologize for taking time to do something you love and/or need to do. Be willing to show yourself and others that writing is a priority in your life, whether you are making money at it or not. (My position is that the money that you make from writing is not the point. It's nice, but it's not the point.)

It is going to happen often enough that life will interrupt

you because it has to. But sometimes it interrupts you only because you let it. Learn to tell the difference, and act accordingly.

Finally, remember this: Dealing with visitors and friends and family can be a lot like dealing with children. If you do not vacillate about what it is you need and what you are going to do, they will have an easier time accepting it. Be honest, firm, and friendly; everyone will be better off. You won't be quietly seething, and neither will they. Well, not about your writing, anyway.

Playground

In your effort to take yourself seriously as a writer, don't forget your need to have fun, too. It's often when I'm doing something for pleasure that I get good ideas for my work.

Remembering to play also means you keep a necessary balance and richness in your life. And the more enriched you are as a person, the better your writing can be. Understand, too, that everything that happens when you're *not* working can be used as material for when you *are*—in that sense, writers are never not working. (In that sense, they can be dangerous to be around, too.)

I once went for a walk under protest with a friend who said—rightly—that I needed to get out more. The first few minutes of that walk, I complained mightily about how I didn't have time to be doing this; then I began to relax. My friend and I ended up lying under some trees, looking at an upside-down blue bowl of a sky, and having a conversation that felt like a long drink of spring water given to someone who hadn't known until she tasted it how thirsty she'd been. It seemed as though pieces of myself that had been lying scattered about in confusion were put back inside me to make a coherent whole. The next day, some vital part nourished, I ended up working better than I had in weeks.

Privacy

Most writers, by nature, need a lot of time by themselves. It's important to write alone, at least some of the time, but I think it's important for us to *be* alone a fair amount of the time, too. Then we can often get rid of a kind of internal scorecard that makes us compare ourselves to others, and that makes us do things according to the way we think others would have us do them. We need the chance to draw from our own unique selves, to act according to our own beliefs, without any interference from others. I believe that solitude, perhaps more than anything, breeds creativity, breeds originality.

Let me put it this way: Think of what happens when you watch a sunset with someone else. Then think of what happens when you watch it alone. Each experience is valuable. But the thing about experiencing things alone is that your own shade is pulled wide open. Your feet are firmly planted on your own ground.

There's another kind of privacy that's important, too, and that's privacy of material.

We all like praise, and we all seek it, even if we don't always do well at accepting it. (Of course that's another story.) When we write something that we think is pretty darn good, almost all of us have a fierce desire to have someone read it *right away* and faint with admiration. Similarly, when we have what we think is a pretty good *idea* for writing something, we might have an urge to tell someone so that they can admire that. My advice is, *Do not tell anyone*. After more than thirteen years of writing for publication, I can say without reservation that the less fully developed an idea is, the less you should talk about it. There's more to this than the possible leak of creative energy. The real problem with talking too much about what you're doing is that you set yourself up for judgment. And if someone sneers at your idea, however subtly they do it, it can cripple you. And they don't even have to sneer—someone simply asking too many questions, pushing you too hard to say what something is before you *know* what it is, can freeze you up.

A scene I witnessed one day will drive this point home. I was sitting in a nursery school classroom, watching two four-year-olds, a boy and a girl, playing side by side at the sand table. Here's their conversation:

> He: What are you making?
> She: (smiles shyly) Something.
> He: (demanding) Let me see.
> She: (softly) No.
> He: Let me see!!
> She: (not softly) NO!!
> He: But what are you *making*?
> She: (walking away) Nothing.

You'll learn when it's time to show or talk about something you're writing—and you'll learn about whom you can trust. But at first, err on the side of caution and discretion.

Proofreaders

When you are finished with something, it really is a good idea to run it past some trusted readers. What you want, when you do that, is for those people to offer you constructive criticism. Well, what you *want* is for them to be rendered speechless because of the dazzling quality of your prose. But if they find something in your work that they don't like, that "doesn't work for them," you presumably want to hear about that, too. As good as it feels to hear that someone likes something (and as necessary), it can actually be more valuable to hear what he or she doesn't like. It can lead you to make changes that improve the material. The key here is that you remember that it has to seem better to *you*.

I think the best thing to do with people who read your work is to encourage them to say all they want to, to provide a climate where they feel safe doing that, and then to take or leave their advice with no hard feelings—on either side. I know this seems obvious; I know I'm presenting it as though it's the easiest, most natural thing in the world. In fact, it's extremely complex, the giving and taking of criticism about writing. Suffice to say that it can be extremely valuable—if not necessary—to solicit others' opinions about your work. Just take care in choosing those whom you ask to look at it; and then be careful of what you do with their advice. I know more than one really fine writer who was savaged by critiques given them at their quite prestigious schools of writing. One gave up writing altogether, damn it; another went on to write a wonderful nonfiction book that sold well *and* got great reviews. I haven't heard a thing about the people who were so eager to put her down.

Playfulness

If there is one thing I would like to have happen to people reading this book, it would be that they would take themselves seriously as writers. That having been said, let me now remind you not to take yourselves *too* seriously! For one thing, it will make you annoying to be around. For another, you will gum up your own works. You will be unable to think of writing as being fun. And writing *is* fun—even if you're writing material that makes your readers—and you—cry.

If you take yourself and writing too seriously, you will sit at your computer and feel afraid to start. When you finally do start, you will be hypercritical of every line you write. If you have a computer glitch and lose some pages, you'll think you can *never* get that stuff back, that you will *never* say it so well again, that the world (and you) are infinitely poorer for it. And yet I've heard stories of writers who bemoaned losing material; then found that they liked better what they did to replace it.

Being too serious also means that if, after all the anguish, you finally publish a book, you'll *continue* the anguish—you'll be unable to enjoy the success: You'll worry about reviews, the next contract, etc.

Learn from the inherent wisdom of children. Watch them when they work: They make it fun. Actually, they try to make everything fun—not for nothing do we have those straws that resemble less a tool for drinking than a plate of spaghetti. And children are *there* when they are there; they are experts at being in the moment.

Love your writing; be there with your writing; respect your writing; but don't sabotage yourself with seriousness. Try to keep some essential perspective: You are not performing an emergency tracheotomy. You are not deciding whether or not to drop the Bomb. You are putting lines of print on a page. And I believe if you're enjoying yourself when you put those lines down, you have a better chance of your readers enjoying you.

Persuasiveness

In some ways, writing is like being a salesperson: You are in the business of convincing someone to buy something, as in, believe something. Try to develop your skills of persuasion so that your villain, say, is really *felt* as a villain. In doing that, think about the small things—everything really *is* in the details. For example, it's not so much the description of the murderer killing someone that demonstrates his evil nature, it's the flatness in his eyes as he does it; it's the way he goes and gets an ice cream immediately afterward. Similarly, a man offering a diamond bracelet to a woman shows love; but that same person smiling tenderly when he wipes the smear of catsup off her face shows more.

In trying to reach your reader, don't fall prey to what I call "dead dog in the road syndrome." What I mean by that is that *anybody* is going to feel terrible if you talk about certain things; what you have to try for is a certain emotional authenticity, an earned reader response. Most of all, remember the first rule when trying to convince a reader of anything: If you don't believe it, neither will they.

Prosperity

Well, maybe not prosperity. But ideally, you need to have enough security that you're not writing for every cent that keeps you fed, housed, and clothed. If you need to sell something, it makes you feel desperate; and that can show in the writing. So try to have a bit of savings you can draw from; or keep your day job until you start making enough money by writing to quit. You really can do both: Get up earlier to write in the morning before you go to work; write during your lunch hour; set aside time at night and on your days off. It will require some sort of sacrifice at first, but if you're meant to be (or in fact already are) a writer, you'll find a way to do it.

Push

Everybody needs a little extra inspiration from time to time. Find out what works as a literary stimulant for you, and use it shamelessly. For some, it's being away from home and in another place—going on a literary retreat, perhaps. For others, it's reading certain things, including the newspaper. I find that reading fiction I admire makes me want to leap up and hit the keys—Alice Munro and Anne Tyler are two authors who really inspire me. So do certain kinds of poetry.

Sometimes a walk outside will stimulate your thinking, or a walk through an art museum, or hanging around a café where there are interesting conversations going on. Listening to certain kinds of music can stimulate your urge to write. I like going to library reference rooms and seeing the myriad subjects one can learn about, walking through the stacks and touching the spines of so many worthy books.

Payoffs

Before the outside rewards of money or praise come, reward yourself for the work you do. Treat yourself as you might a favorite child—promise yourself something if certain conditions are met, and then make sure you follow through. It can be a very small reward: I know one writer who won't eat her breakfast until she completes five pages. On the other hand, I know another writer who, when she sold her last novel, bought a BMW. There are lots of notches in between these two points—"giving" yourself a movie, a large-size Hershey's bar, a new sweater. The point is, it can feel great to try for a prize and then get it, even if you're working both sides of the booth. And a reward system works well to keep you coming back for more.

Pride

This is a tricky thing, because there are a lot of writers or would-be writers out there who don't have a problem in the world with pride. But there are also some very sensitive souls who *should* have pride about their work; but they have a very difficult time letting themselves have anything. This message is for them:

Listen to me. You need to be a home for yourself and your work. You need to be the safe place to present things to be admired and loved. Never mind what anyone else has to say about your work, be it good or bad. Know that it's necessary that *you* love your work, and let yourself do that. Relish what you are doing; whether you succeed or fail in the eyes of the outer world has nothing to do with the fact that you are answering a calling and making art as best you can. The world is rich because of people who do what you do. Treat yourself and your pages with respect—you know how to do it. Do not think you cannot call yourself a writer until you've been published.

Pens, Pencils, and Paper

This is a very good way to indulge yourself. Go to a gigantic office supply store and spend a long time looking at all the options available to you, and get the ones that make you feel the best. You also need a dictionary, a thesaurus, and a guide to good grammar. A nice extra is a copy of the current *Writer's Market*.

Patience

Sometimes the well runs dry. Sometimes it takes longer than usual for an agent or an editor to respond to you. Understand that there are going to be times when there's nothing to do but wait. Move on to the next project, or find the joy in being idle for a while.

You will probably be relieved to know that I have a couple of things to say about getting started that do not start with the letter P. Except by general classification. Let's call these things "peripherals":

I believe there are three things you need to do to get published:

Have something to say.

This needs to be something that would interest someone outside yourself, something that has some inherent interest, or resonance. Mike Curtis, fiction editor at *Atlantic Monthly*, once described worthwhile content as being something you would tell someone in a car. I think of it as being a story that might begin with "Hey, you know what?" or "Listen to this," a story that more or less has a beginning, a middle, and an end—and a point. People also like a story that makes them *feel* something.

Say it well.

It's probably not a good idea to bypass basic rules of grammar, especially when you're first starting out. There are times when work is presented in a purposefully grammatically incorrect way, but the author's control shows through. It's much like when Victor Borge plays the piano.

Also, remember that there really *is* an art to telling a story. Think of people who tell jokes well: What do they do that holds the interest of their listeners? Consider their characterizations, the tension they put into the drama, the ability they have to make things seem believable, the way they save the best for last.

Send it out.

No matter how good you are, nobody is going to come knocking at your door. You have to take the risk of rejection, and get that material out there. Assume, as much as possible, that it *might* get taken, not that it *must* be. Also, be aware that just because a piece is rejected, it does not necessarily mean that the idea or the writing is bad.

One last thing. When it comes to writing, please remember that nothing is wasted. *Nothing* is wasted. It may be that you can lift whole paragraphs out of pieces you've written to put into something else, or that you can use lines of dialogue you've written for one piece in another.

It can happen that although the execution of an idea didn't work, the basic idea is still good, and you can try it another way successfully. Even in a worst case scenario where you don't feel anything is worth saving, you still got valuable practice time in.

Homework

I have spent considerable time in this chapter telling you that you don't need to spend a lot of money to get started writing. However, I would like you to spend *some*. People tend to value things they pay for. So I want you to go shopping for yourself as a writer. Today (or tomorrow, if you can't go today), go and buy yourself the most beautiful large-size blank book you can afford. Look for it in an art store, a bookstore, an office supply store, or a stationery store. You'll know which one to get—it will speak to you.

Use this bound book for the writing assignments that will be given here. Use it for recording dreams. Use it to paste in *anything* that strikes your fancy: photos, pressed flowers, a newspaper article, found objects. Keep it close by you, especially when you sleep. Pull, *uncensored*, anything that's in your mind that you want to record, whether it's fact or fiction. You may not, *under any circumstances*, show *anyone* what is in your book. Nor may you edit what's in it. If there is something that you simply must show (or submit to) someone, copy it onto another piece of paper and show him or her that.

The reason for not showing the book (you might even consider buying a book that locks, or keeping your book in a locked place) is so that there is an external safe place for your writing, even as there should be an internal one. We all need safe places; and I believe we can all profit from a little rich secrecy, especially the kind that is held inside ourselves.

We need to nourish and encourage our creative selves, and we need to learn to take chances. The best way to do that is to have a place where there is no judgment, where anything goes. As we get older, it can be harder and harder to find those places. We have to create them for ourselves.

> I carry a brick on my shoulder, in order that
> the world may know what my house was like.
> —BERTOLT BRECHT

*When I decided to do a book on writing, one of the people I
told about my plan was Eileen Jordan. Eileen is a beautiful
blue-eyed woman who is a study in elegance, grace, and generosity. I had the good fortune to work with her when she was
an editor at* Woman's Day *magazine, where she bought a
number of essays from me. (She is now herself a wonderful
freelance writer of fiction and nonfiction—you can find her
byline in many magazines.) Eileen said she was really happy I
was doing a book on writing, and that she would be my first
reader. She also said, "If you could translate your wonderful
ability to make it look easy, you would win the lottery."*

*Consider this chapter my attempt to share my ways, in the
hope that you can learn to find writing easy, or at least less
like work and more like play. Consider it also my attempt to
win the lottery.*

I was once asked to speak to a group of women taking a
writing class at Radcliffe. There were two other writers
there as well who were sisters. When the usual questions

arose about methods for writing, and I described mine, one sister whispered to the other, "Well, but see, she's a *natural.*"

I know that writing does not come as easily to everyone as it does to me; I know that not everyone finds it as joyful a process as I do, either. But I also know that many people can write in a much more authentic voice than they do, and that just as many seem to be trying much harder than they have to. What I want to look at in this chapter is why you should attempt to write in your own voice; then how you might go about doing exactly that.

One of my favorite scenes in a movie happens when a man comes upon a woman washing dishes and singing— loudly and off-key. She doesn't know she's being observed. She simply scrubs the plates and sings, swaying her butt back and forth in a little sinkside dance; and in her decidedly imperfect singing, she communicates her perfect happiness. The man leans against the doorjamb, arms crossed, watching her, and as you watch him, you understand why he has come to love her.

The people who are the most irresistible are those who are most themselves. It's not an easy thing to be your true self—all of us feel compelled to live up to certain standards, to achieve a certain level of status, to fit in, or, even better, to be cool. We all suffer from a certain amount (sometimes a *great* amount) of insecurity. But there is something so charismatic about someone being wholeheartedly and unaffectedly themselves. It's one of the reasons young children are so charming. It's one of the reasons the television show *Candid Camera*, which "caught people in the act of being themselves," was so successful.

The inherent appeal in people being themselves holds true even for marginal types or outright bad guys—you may not want them over for dinner or to baby-sit for your children, but you still feel drawn to them in a certain way; often, in fact, you are absolutely mesmerized by them. (Did you take your eyes off Hannibal Lecter in *The Silence of the Lambs*?)

This attraction to people being themselves is good news for writers. It means that we can present virtually any type of character, and so long as they are truly rendered, a reader is likely to be interested in them.

But how is it that a character is truly rendered? Or a scene, or a feeling, or a time in history? Well, one way is by writing from a true place, which comes from writing in a natural voice. But how do you do that?

Maybe the answer can best be found in how *not* to do it.

I have a friend who is the most wonderfully well-spoken man imaginable. He can tell you a simple story about a mockingbird he saw on one of his walks and make the hairs on the back of your neck rise up, make your cynical heart soften. He has a lilting rhythm in his speech, a respectful, loving, and thoughtful view of life; a deep intelligence; an incredible sensitivity; and a frankly poetic way of stringing words together. But when he writes, all of that is lost. What he puts down on the page is affected, unfocused, difficult to get through—ultimately irritating. Why? What happens in the translation?

The truth is, I'm not exactly sure. But I have some ideas.

For one thing, when this man sits down at his computer to write, his whole physical being changes. I've seen it.

Tension surrounds him like an aura: He sits up too straight, clears his throat, licks his lips, takes in a deep breath as though he is preparing himself for execution. He types a line. Then he leans close in to scrutinize it, thinks about whether or not every word in it is right, if something could or should be changed. Rather than simply sitting down to literally transfer the things he says out loud onto paper, he changes them. He tries to put them into some arbitrary form that he thinks the written word must have, and in so doing, he kills those beautiful words and ideas dead.

To write naturally, using your own voice, try to think of what you are doing as dictation. Put down onto the paper the words you are hearing in your head—literally. And do not act as editor at the same time that you are being the writer. It is vitally important that you keep those two roles entirely separate.

First, only write. When you're all done writing, go have a snack or take a walk or goof off in some way for a while—get some space between you and what you've done. *Then* edit.

You've probably heard "Keep the editor off your shoulder" before. But I'll say it again, because it's very, very important. And I would add something. I would say not only should you keep your editor off your shoulder, you should keep your *self* off your shoulder. Write in as unself-conscious a way as you can. Write like you tie your shoes—don't think about it, just do it. Maxwell Perkins probably said it best when he said, "You have to throw yourself away when you write."

There's more to writing naturally than trying to avoid affectation in your presentation. There is also a need for a certain kind of honesty in the material you're trying to present.

I believe that one of your most important jobs as a writer is to be true to yourself, to honor your own notions of what you believe is important to your life and to that of others. If you love history, use it in your work. If you love mystery, do the same. I'm sure you've also heard, countless times, "Write what you know." I would change that to "Write what you love." The knowledge can be learned; the passion can't be—it's either there or it isn't.

So. Say you like writing about people in contemporary times, and you like to focus on relationships—relationships between husbands and wives, in particular. If that is the subject you like to write about, it's likely that's what you like to read about, too. But if you are writing about a marriage in trouble, for example, avoid reading things that deal with marriages in trouble until you finish your own work. This will keep you writing from your own thoughts and feelings, from your own point of view.

It's much too seductive to read someone else writing about what you are, when you are writing it. You may think you're reading others "just to get some ideas" or "just to study technique"; you may think you are fully aware of the difference between being inspired by something and copying it. But no matter how aware or sophisticated or experienced you are, no matter how determined to write your own story, there's a very real danger that you *will* start to copy. It may be unconscious, but it can happen. And if that happens, it's a shame.

It's a shame because it's copying, which is lazy and unethical; and it's a shame because it denies the reading public the pleasure of your originality. If you are influenced by someone else's description of a grandmother when you write about your own, you don't draw fully from your own rich resources. So your grandmother wasn't a scintillating figure who greatly influenced the art world of the thirties. Your grandmother lived on a farm in Indiana and wore socks that slid down into pink sneakers. You never saw her without an apron. She kept little hard candies in her pockets, and she doled them out to grandchildren—and to the baby pigs in the spring. Also, she could put her fingers in her mouth and whistle as loud as any man. Is her life any less interesting? Not to me. And not to many others.

You know the phrase "It's always the little things"? In writing, it *is* always the little things—it's the details, and the authenticity in those details, that make a character and a story come alive. And it's your eye seeing and writing those details in the most natural way you can that means you are writing in your own voice. Get out of your own way and let the story happen.

But how do you get out of your own way, really, get your self off your shoulder? How do you become less self-conscious and more accepting of your own creative process? I can only describe it as a leap of faith, a process of letting go and giving yourself over to an inner guide. It's a lot like falling in love, that scary letting go and learning to trust in something outside yourself. But once that kind of trust is achieved, something else, something deep inside you, takes over when you write. It is at that point when you really do begin to feel that you are just the typist. And it is at that point when you start to feel terrific, because honestly, it feels like magic. I think it probably is.

Now. All that having been said, it will still happen some-times that your entirely original material turns out to be greatly similar to someone else's, in one way or another. For example, just after I had turned in my manuscript for *The Pull of the Moon,* which is about a fifty-year-old woman running away from home, I read about a book Anne Tyler had just released, which was about the same thing. I remember sitting in a chair and reading about *Ladder of Years* and feeling sick to my stomach. Anne Tyler, no less! I went out and bought the book and read it (which I would have done anyway, since I like her so much). And I found, to my vast relief, that her book was really nothing like mine.

Still, it does happen that writers can end up creating things that are very similar. If you subscribe to the belief that everything's already been said, that should come as no surprise. But there are myriad ways of saying things, which brings me back to the importance of writing in your own voice. Every individual, amazingly, really is unique. There-fore, every individual has something unique to offer. When it comes to writing, you'll see the singular aspect of an author made manifest not so much in what he or she says, but in how they say it.

If you want to write in a natural way, remember that there's no need to guild the lily. Some people seem to think that writ-ing requires things being presented in a larger-than-life way. But the old adage of less being more is almost always true. Don't overwrite a story that is inherently interesting—it adds nothing but clutter.

Here's an example: Imagine the proud father of a new-born being left in charge of that baby. He's told his wife not to worry about a thing; the baby's just been fed, she's sound asleep, what could happen? The wife is at the door ready to go out when the husband flicks on the television, only to have both parents see a news story about a school bus that overturned, killing all thirty children on board. The man and his wife go instantly to stand at the side of the crib, where they watch the baby sleep. Then the father pulls the blanket up higher over the baby, stands back, and takes his wife's hand.

Everything that man feels is in those gestures. He doesn't have to say that he fears for his baby, that he wants her life to be perfect, even while there is gruesome acknowledgment in him that life is not perfect at all, even for young children. He just has to stand there, feeling what he does. The writer has to be there with him, also feeling what he does, and making him do only what is necessary to have the reader feel it, too. That's how life is—at the times when we feel the most, we often say the least. Again, it's the little details that speak for us. And your involvement as a writer in showing the reader those details needs to be heartfelt and well considered, but minimal.

That's because there is a certain kind of resistance a reader feels when he or she is being told to feel a certain way. A passage that is too ornate, too overwrought, says to the reader, "*Look* at this! Do you see how *sad* this is? (Or funny, or grim, or scary?) A reader likes to do a little work, to make his or her own discoveries. And most readers are much smarter than some writers—and editors—believe. Nuance works. Subtlety works. Make the act of someone reading you an interactive process by expecting that reader to bring a level of willingness and acceptance–and imagination—to you. Lure, don't force, readers into a story with you. Remember that they *want* to be lured, they want to lose themselves in your words.

Overwriting is irritating to read because oftentimes it's a way a writer has of showing off, and of making herself too much present in her own material. Most readers want a kind of intimacy only between themselves and what's being written about, whether it's fiction or nonfiction.

When you're trying to write naturally, the most important thing to do is to relax. I know that this is easy to say and quite possibly very hard to do. I suppose it might be like a team of surgeons leaning over a patient on the OR table, and telling *him* to relax.

Perhaps the best way for me to try to explain what I mean is to ask you to consider how you walk. You don't plan ahead and think about every move. If you had to think about it, it would be very difficult, indeed—how is it that we even keep our balance? But if you can assume, as I do, that there is something inside you that already knows how to write naturally, that you wouldn't be drawn to write unless that thing were in place, that it is a kind of instinct with which you were born—well, then you're off and running.

Try to be ever observant, to look beyond surfaces. Let yourself feel everything that you can. When you listen to the way people talk, hear the phrasing, the accent, the pauses, the pacing, the words beneath the words. As a writer, you should have a sticky soul; the act of continually taking things in should be as much a part of you as your hair color.

Well. We now come to the New Age part of the chapter. For those of you who eschew Tarot cards, aromatherapy, and encouraging what we shall call, for lack of a better term, "woo-woo" experiences, I'm sorry. But I believe in messages from the universe, however you define it, and I believe part of writing in your own voice is trusting in it. And part of trusting in the universe is asking for guidance from it, then accepting that guidance (or reassurance) when it comes. Let me illustrate my point this way.

When I first conceived of writing this book, it was because something inside me was resisting starting the next novel. When I thought about writing more fiction, I felt a little tired. But when I thought about a book on writing, I felt invigorated. For me, the choice was clear.

Still, after I committed to writing this book, I became anxious about abandoning fiction, even temporarily. I sat in my study one day, worrying, thinking, *Oh, I don't know if this is the right decision.* I decided to read some good fiction, to see if I felt drawn into doing that instead. I picked up a book of Edna O'Brien's. In her introduction, I read a very wise thing about—guess what?—writing. What she said was, "Writing is a matter of wakeful dreaming."

This statement is something with which I couldn't agree more. It is also exactly the kind of thing I would like to pass along to anyone who wants to write. Out of all the fiction books I might have picked up, I ended up with this one. For me, this was a message, a strong indication that I should return to my original idea. It put me back on course to finish a project that really *was* a good idea for me.

I think that other "signs" have to do with things as subtle

as a general feeling of well-being when you're writing. If what you're doing is somehow wrong for you, I believe you'll feel that, too—and you should pay attention to it.

A few last words to help you in learning to write in your own unique voice. Remember that, schools of writing notwithstanding, *there is no formula*. (This is actually good. It means there's nothing to memorize or get quizzed on, no standard outside yourself for you to hold yourself up against.)

There is, in fact, no single right way to do anything in writing. There is just the desire to communicate something on paper, and the fact of it then "working" or not. Be very, very wary of the words "always" and "never," both in your life in general and in the craft of writing in particular. People will tell you with great authority never to do this and never to do that and then you will read a book that is ecstatically praised for breaking all the rules. People will tell you to always do this and always do that and then they will criticize your work for being too predictable. Well, jeez. I wonder why.

When you're writing, worry only about how you feel about what's appearing on the page, not the opinions of others you've heard talking about writing. Consider only this: What are you trying to say? How does it feel, the way you are trying to say it? Does it feel right? Does it please you?

That's it. No one else should be in your head when you write—not your editor, not your lover, not your readers. Neither should you be worried about any aspect of publishing—will this sell? be well reviewed? That's all pollution.

First, honor your own original impulses. Get the thing written in the way that you want to write it. Then worry about business aspects. Or, better yet, let your agent worry about them.

Homework

The Reckless Writer

Go and get your journal. (Remember that journal I told you to buy? Did you think I was kidding? I wasn't kidding.) Think of some event that happened in your life that made a real emotional impact on you. It can be any emotion—anger, fear, sadness, nostalgia—but let yourself remember the event fully, so that you can feel the emotion all over again.

Now set a timer for ten minutes and write—very, very quickly—from that place of feeling. Use first person, present tense. Draw on all your senses: sight, hearing, taste, touch, smell. Do not work up to how this event occurred; do not consider what it meant or how any aspect of it might appear to other people; just jump right in the middle, with it happening to you. Do not chew on your pen and ponder what to say after the first sentence. Keep that pen moving the whole time. Focus not on what you just said, but on what you are going to say next. Tell the page like you would tell a person, and keep telling until the timer goes off. Then stop. You may not write any longer than ten minutes. (This is for a reason that will be revealed to you later.)

4 *If You're a Man, Be a Woman:*
Exercises to Unleash Your Creativity

> The greatest thing a human soul ever does in
> this world is to *see* something, and tell what it
> saw in a plain way.
>
> —JOHN RUSKIN

This chapter is full of a variety of exercises designed to help you see, and hear, and feel—to access and utilize all of your senses, in fact. Doing these exercises will also help teach you that less is more; that it is far more effective to show than to tell; that writing realistic dialogue has much to do with the art of listening; and that thinking less and writing more can become a very good habit.

As much as possible, do these assignments quickly. Don't try to think of a "right" answer—there are none. Just write whatever comes into your head, even if it doesn't "make sense." What you're doing is priming the subconscious pump—you don't want a standard, logical answer; rather, you want to be surprised, entertained, and intrigued. If you're thinking too hard, you won't feel any of those things—you'll feel only a homework headache. Besides, sometimes the things that at fist glance don't make sense end up being the most valuable: They may in and of themselves be the richest material you've come up with, or they may inspire you to come up with something else that is far more creative—and pleasing—than you might have imagined.

On a given day, you may feel like doing just a few exercises; on another day, you may want to do more—even all of them. It's a good idea to do a number of these assignments before proceeding on to the next chapter, but it is not necessary to do all of them. Please consider completing them all eventually, however. If you let yourself stay open and willing to try new things, it's possible that you'll happily astonish yourself with your responses.

It may happen that a certain exercise strikes a nerve with you, and you'll feel compelled to take it further, or off in an entirely different direction than what was suggested. If you should feel that impulse, by all means, give in to it. Work on it for as long as you like; then come back to the chapter.

Make sure you do these exercises in your journal. At this stage, it's important for you to keep everything you create. When your experience as a writer grows, you'll be better able to decide what really can get thrown out. But for now, keep it all.

Every time you have finished doing the number of exercises you want to, read over your work. When you have come up with something you particularly like, highlight it in some way, either by using markers, or by boxing or underlining it. This will make a particular piece of writing easier to find, either for the pleasure of rereading work of your own that you really like, or in case you want to use it again somewhere else.

The presentation of these exercises is purposefully chaotic. You might find short fill-in-the-blank phrases next to exercises for dialogue, which may be next to a kind of guided meditation, which may be next to a single word meant to evoke something—anything!—in you. There are a few reasons for this. For one thing, it's good practice to write not knowing what's going to come next. For another, spontaneity is by definition created by encountering the unexpected.

Perhaps most important, though, is a certain dullness of spirit that comes when you do too much of one thing; and if there is anything that this chapter is meant to do, it's to keep you alert and interested. Your mission is to find and enlarge upon your own writer's voice, your literary fingerprint. That is what will set you apart from other writers, and let you come up with the phrasing of which only you are capable.

A bit about technique. When you encounter a fill-in-the-blank, you may use it as is, or you may expand or rearrange it. Consider "_____ Christmas trees." This blank may be filled in with "Dickensian" or "martyred" or "snow-frosted" or a million other things; or you may write something like, "tossed-away Christmas trees, lying forlornly at the curb," or "Christmas trees, arboreal porcupines." The important thing, again, is to honor whatever impulse comes first, and then let it live in the pages of your *private* journal.

When you come across an isolated phrase, do with it whatever you like, whatever comes to you, fiction or nonfiction. "First kiss," for example, may inspire a sentence, a paragraph, or notes that are the germ of a novel. The phrase may also inspire a stream of consciousness such as *Jerry D, "Theme from a Summer Place," hot summer night, smell of* aftershave, unexpected softness of a boy's neck, pointy black flats.

The exercises in this chapter can be done over and over again. You can create so many different moods and meanings by your selection of words, whether you're writing a long essay inspired by the phrase "my father's hands" or by putting one simple adjective next to one simple noun. The world of choice in writing is vast and invigorating, challenging and joyful. Start these exercises now, and see for yourself. (I will make *very* few suggestions with the first few, which you may use as inspiration or ignore: After that, you're on your own.)

Exercises

◡ *The perfect lunch for lovers: wine, cheese, and*

_____.

(bare knees?)

◡ *Through the window of a Laundromat, you see a woman folding underwear. Describe her. (Face? Clothes? Hands? Vocalizations?)*

◡ *getting a puppy (joys and frustrations, first night)*

◡ *a flock of geese,* _____*ing*

◡ *black* _____

◡ *calm as* _____

ↄ *If you are a man, describe how it feels to have "too small" breasts. If you are a woman, voice the frustrations of having an inadequate-size penis. Use first person: If you're a man, "be" a woman, if you're a woman, "be" a man.*

ↄ *Use these three words in a sentence or brief paragraph: snowman, pink, window.*

ↄ *Describe three kinds of rain.*

ლ ლ ლ

ↄ *You are given a dollar, and told to use it to buy a gift for someone very important to you. What do you buy, and for whom?*

ↄ *putting a child to sleep*

ↄ *situation: A nurse walks into a room to take care of a patient and abruptly discovers that he/she was her/his lover for a brief time, thirty years ago. In dialogue only, write the first few things these people say to each other. Use no description, no "he said" or "she said," just use straight lines of dialogue.*

ↄ *your first job*

ↄ *curly as* _____

ѡ *true as* _____

ѡ _____ *as milk*

ѡ *You see a child doing something in a schoolyard at recess that makes you stop and watch for a long time. What is the child doing, and what makes you want to watch?*

ѡ *Your teenage daughter gets rejected by her first real flame.*

ѡ *kind as* _____

ѡ _____ *as a witch*

ѡ _____ *rivers*

ѡ *your mother: "There was something I always wanted from you, and that was* _____*."*

ѡ *In the lines of her face, I saw* _____.

ѡ *your grandmother's house on a holiday*

ѡ *Walking past a restaurant, you get a whiff of a certain kind of food, which brings back strong memories. What is the food? In a stream-of-consciousness way, present the memories.*

ဖ *Can you go home again? Why or why not?*

ဖ *If you're a man, describe the onset of menstruation. If you're a woman, write about how it feels the first time you experience a wet dream.*

ဖ *Write a description of two completely different kinds of feet.*

ဖ *Using one character and no dialogue, write a brief scene that occurs in each room of your house. The scene should tell the reader something definitive about the character.*

໑ ໑ ໑

ဖ *Make up and describe a family and a house for the person who delivers your newspaper.*

ဖ _____ *children*

ဖ _____ *Christmas trees*

ဖ _____ *like Mamie Eishenhower's*

ဖ *terrible in its* _____

ဖ *Compare happiness to an animal.*

◡ *Envision a town and its inhabitants, your own Lake Wobegon. Now describe the eccentric mailman there.*

◡ _____ *anger*

◡ _____ *white*

◡ *falling* _____

◡ *Use these three words in a sentence or brief paragraph: dream, heart, gold.*

◡ *the best time of day; the worst time of day*

◡ *a road trip on a motorcycle*

ᦔ ᦔ ᦔ

◡ *After reading this description, write out the scene: You are visiting the grave of someone about whom you had very strong feelings. While there, you suddenly begin talking out loud. The words you say make you realize something you never understood before. Before leaving, you put something on the grave.*

◡ _____ *sadness*

◡ *leashed dogs,* _____*ing*

◡ *the perfect partner for you would* _____

۵ _____ as Tarzan

۵ *If you are a man, write about what it feels like to have
a baby. If you are a woman, write about how it feels to
learn you've impregnated someone.*

෨ ෨ ෨ ෨

۵ *You are driving along when a song comes on the radio
that brings back strong memories. What's the song?
What are the memories?*

۵ *He's so weird! He likes to eat* _____ *and*
_____ *together.*

۵ *Pick up a random novel and turn to a random
paragraph. Write a new first and last sentence for that
paragraph.*

۵ *the* _____ *of children, just out of school*

۵ _____ *as whiskers*

۵ *grouped like* _____

۵ *losing a pet to an accident; to old age*

۵ *Write—quickly!—a five-sentence paragraph
backward. In other words, start with the last sentence,
and end with the first.*

ᴈ *The line of dialogue is "I told you!" By including
physical details, describe a person saying this in a scary
way. A sad way. A self-satisfied way. An angry way.
A happy way. A frustrated way. A defeated way.*

ᴈ *Something about the situation seemed off, as when
you add what you think is sugar to your coffee, only to
find that it's* _____ .

ᴈ _____ *as New Orleans*

ᴈ *hot as a* _____ *on a* _____

ᴈ *innocent as* _____

ᴈ *the worst date you ever had*

ᘒ ᘒ ᘒ

ᴈ *If you're a woman, write a scene of one man telling
another how best to attract a woman. If you're a man,
write what one woman would tell another about how
best to attract a man.*

ᴈ *You are looking out a hotel window in New York City.
What do you see? hear? taste? smell? Now you are at
the edge of a desert; now in the Pacific Ocean;
climbing a mountain; standing on a flat plain in
Nebraska; on a small town's street at Christmas time;
in a glorious cathedral; in a tiny chapel.*

ɿ _Write the first line for a love story._

ɿ _Write the last line for a tragedy._

ɿ _summer of '67_

ɿ _relaxed as_ _____

ɿ _____ _fear_

ɿ _____ _water_

ɿ _what people's desk drawers say about them_

ɿ _Write a brief (three to four sentences) scene featuring you and the following people (the scenes need not be related):_

    your mother, your grandmother, your sister, and your daughter (If you don't have some of these people in your life, make them up.)

    your father, your grandfather, your brother, and your son (If you don't have some of these people in your life, make them up.)

ɿ _You are given a box of clothes from someone extremely close to you who died suddenly. Write a scene of your sorting through these clothes._

∽ Use these three words in a short paragraph: bus, smoke, zipper.

∽ the music of the Rolling Stones

∽∾ ∽∾ ∽∾

∽ Write a paragraph (or a story) relating three disparate objects, such as a license plate, a star, and a chickadee.

∽ rings of _____

∽ holding tightly to his _____

∽ the _____ shade of the trees

∽ If you're a man, write a description of what a woman wants in a good woman friend. If you're a woman, describe what a man wants in a good man friend.

∽ Write a brief story that you would really love to see in the newspaper.

∽ Using these words to launch you, continue with streams of consciousness: airplane, bread, diary.

∽ Describe the smells in these places: a church, a hospital waiting room, a public bathroom, a library.

ᴗ A young couple is moving into a house where an old widower is moving out. What does he tell them?

ᴗ Describe a scene by starting with a wide-angle view, then moving in for a close-up. Now do the opposite.

ᴗ What is a grandiose idea you had as a child? (Here's an example: A friend of mine thought he could hold the Winter Olympics in his tiny backyard, and he was going to invite the Queen of England. His only concern was what to do with the little kids in his large family when Her Highness ate dinner in his kitchen—he didn't want them at the table spilling their milk.)

ᴗ What were some totally inaccurate ideas or beliefs you had as a child? (I believed there were tiny cast-iron pots in my stomach, one for each variety of food that I ate. I worried constantly about them overflowing and killing me.)

ꝏ ꝏ ꝏ

ᴗ Go to a restaurant and watch someone for ten minutes. Write down every single thing he or she does. (Try not to get caught, as it could be embarrassing.)

ᴗ Describe dinner with your family when you were a child in contrast to what it's like now.

ა *Write a suicide's note.*

ა *a screen door, slamming*

ა *your grandmother's bathroom*

ა *bright as* _____

ა _____ *cities*

ა _____ *layers*

ა *crumbs of chocolate cake,* _____ *on his face*

ა _____ *rise of* _____ *hills*

ა *If you're a woman, write what a man would say if asked to describe the best meal imaginable, from appetizer to dessert. If you're a man, imagine what a woman would say if asked to do the same.*

∽ ∽ ∽

ა *What is your biggest regret?*

ა *Find a poem you like. Make a story out of it—one paragraph or many pages.*

ა *Describe a child sucking her thumb; now an adult doing the same.*

᠊ᢒ Write a scene featuring a brother and sister washing dishes peacefully together.

᠊ᢒ As a child, how did you play house? war? dolls? school?

∾ ∾ ∾

᠊ᢒ What's extraordinary about an ordinary day?

᠊ᢒ I knew he was upset, because for dinner he had eaten
_____.

᠊ᢒ If I could create a job for myself, it would be _____.

᠊ᢒ Write a brief love scene with these characters: two very old people; two obese people; two people with huge age differences.

᠊ᢒ Show how a good deed can backfire.

᠊ᢒ List four places in the body where you can see fear. Now list three places where you can feel it.

᠊ᢒ Describe the contents of a refrigerator of a very rich person; a very poor person; a crazy person; three kids who have just gotten their first apartment.

᠊ᢒ Write a scene showing these people fighting: two siblings; two lovers; a parent and young child.

◡ *Write what one who wants a long-time relationship says; then the surprising response of his/her partner.*

◡ *Your child has left home for college. What do you find forgotten under the mattress?*

෨ ෨ ෨

◡ *Describe, in detail, a newborn baby.*

◡ *You are having a party and have to include people who are extremely different from one another. Whom do you invite?*

◡ *Your father begins by saying, "It's time to tell you something." Finish what he says.*

◡ *the one who got away*

◡ *Make yourself any age and write this scene: You come upon your mother sitting on her bed, carefully and slowly sifting through the contents of a cigar box. She doesn't see you. What's in the box, and what does she do with those things? How do you feel, watching her?*

◡ *Three characters from your past come to you and say they want you to write about them. Who are they, and why do they want you to write about them?*

- *what you used to love about summer*

- *The best holiday is ________________. Why?*

- *Put on some classical music that you've never heard. Write to it, telling the story that you hear in the music.*

- *the thing you are most ashamed of*

- *mad as ______________________*

- *easy as ______________________*

- *light through her lace curtains, __________ as __________.*

- *Describe a walk on a winter night, including what you see in people's windows.*

- *the wildest thing you ever did*

- *There are three people in the hospital room of a person who is very ill: the doctor, the patient, and the patient's beloved. A crow appears on the windowsill and caws three times, then flies away. What do each of these three people think as they witness this event?*

ᴗ Go to a bar and record exactly a conversation you hear between two people. Include every "uh," "um," "like," and "you know."

ᴗ Launch a tirade: Say everything you want to someone you've been afraid to say anything to.

ᴗ Use these three words in a sentence or a short paragraph: symphony, shoe, television.

ᴗ Thoughts of a man buying lingerie. Thoughts of a woman doing the same.

ᴗ Compare hair to a body of water.

ᴗ a forty-seven-year-old virgin's reflections

ᴗ Who did the old lady with ten cats used to be?

ᴗ Describe a sorrowful wedding day.

ᴗ Describe an amusing funeral.

ᴗ Write an entertaining version of a recipe.

ᴗ the most interesting thing that ever happened at a party

ᴗ Carefully observe every single part of an insect. What do you see? Does it resemble anything else?

ↄ A married couple go into a symphony together. Afterward, without having spoken a word, they know their marriage is over. Describe what happened during the symphony that made them know this.

ↄ A wife is jealous of a woman on TV whom her husband greatly admires. While the couple is out to dinner, they begin fighting about it. Write the scene, using an equal mix of dialogue and physical detail.

ↄↄ ↄↄ ↄↄ

ↄ Write an erotic scene that takes place in a laundry room.

ↄ The man is not crying, but you know his heart is breaking. How do you know?

ↄ A mother and her forty-nine-year-old daughter have a conversation while they are washing dishes after Thanksgiving dinner. What do they say?

ↄ If you're a man, write how a woman would describe the ideal man. If you're a woman, tell how a man would describe his ideal woman. Make this a conversation between two people, and set it in a bar.

ↄ While on a walk, you hear something strange and turn to see a man hiding in the bushes at the side of a house. He says something to you. What is the man doing, what does he say, and how do you respond?

ᴥ Write a scene of someone commandeering an ice-cream store because he was delivered a totally inadequate hot fudge sundae. He leaps over the counter and makes his own sundae, loudly narrating what he believes is the right way to do it.

ᴥ Describe how to write a love letter.

ᴥ something surprising you find in a pocket

ᴥᴥ ᴥᴥ ᴥᴥ

ᴥ Your blind date takes you to his apartment to see his/her pet. Surprise! It's a _____. Describe your reaction.

ᴥ _____ longing

ᴥ red berries on the bush, nature's _____

ᴥ the _____ memory of her _____

ᴥ If you're a woman, describe how a seventeen-year-old boy dresses for a date he's really excited about. If you're a man, describe a young woman doing the same. Use first person, present tense.

ᴥ Describe taking a walk in winter using sounds only.

ᴥ Compare a maple leaf with three other things.

∽ *dream car*

∽ *If you're a man, write about being a woman losing her virginity. If you're a woman, write about a man doing the same.*

∽ *the first time you smoked a cigarette*

∽ *If you could undo one experience in your life, what would it be?*

∽ *You give a dollar to a homeless person who looks up at you and says, "I know you!" Who is the person and how does he or she know you?*

∽ *what used to live under your bed*

∽ *Demonstrate great wrath in a person by describing only the way he or she is smoking a cigarette. Now great fear. Now sorrow.*

∽∾ ∽∾ ∽∾

∽ *Write a conversation where no one is saying what they really mean. (Contrast their body language with their verbal language.)*

∽ *You stare into the grass, close up. What do you see?*

∽ *Compare snow to food.*

ᴥ *If you have ever written a piece of fiction, recall a*
   character you used. Now imagine that character
   coming to you, and telling you what you left out about
   him/her. What does your character say?

ᴥ *What is something you once did that you thought*
   was no big deal, only to find out that it was a huge
   deal?

∾ ∾ ∾

ᴥ *If you're a man, describe a woman's pleasures in*
   shopping; if you're a woman, describe a man's joy
   at watching football.

ᴥ *How does one know when one is truly comfortable*
   with a new lover?

ᴥ *What I always wanted most was his* _____.

ᴥ _____ *knuckles*

ᴥ *an odd smell, a mix of* _____ *and* _____

ᴥ _____ *hunger*

ᴥ *We all huddled together that* _____ *day, like*
   _____ *at a* _____.

ᴥ *the* _____ *of the wishbone*

 ७ *Name three things an ear looks like.*

 ७ *Write a beginning of a short story that is at least half a page long. In three days, without looking at the first version, write the same beginning. Now compare the two versions. Are they much different? Is one better than the other?*

 ७ *an experience of shoplifting*

 ७ *combing the hair of a baby, a very old person, your lover*

 ७ *an unfair punishment you endured*

 ७ *Go to the art museum and find a painting that is particularly evocative. Seated before it, write the story it suggests.*

 ७ *Also at the art museum: Write down five titles of paintings that you believe could be used as titles for a short story or a novel.*

 ७ *You are at a cancer support group meeting. Why? Describe how the other people in the group look. What does the first speaker say?*

 ७ *Find a human interest story in the newspaper. Use it as the basis for a short story, and write out the rough idea for the story, or the story itself.*

ᴖ *Pen a long overdue letter.*

ᴖ *List five adjectives for the way skin feels.*

ᴖ *the best Christmas you remember; the worst*

ᴖ *You are on an airplane that suddenly loses altitude.
Oxygen masks drop; you are told to brace yourself for
an emergency landing. Your seatmate begins laughing
loudly. When you look over at him, what does he say?*

ᴖ *What transpires as you stand before the monkey cage
at the zoo?*

෨ ෨ ෨

ᴖ *Write a scene of these people making dinner together.
What do they prepare, and what do they say to each
other as they prepare it?*

    two boys, age ten

    *two eighty-five-year-olds who have been married for
sixty-five years*

    a couple on their first date

    a cat and a dog

    an alien and an earthling

ᴐ Two cellmates in prison are lying on their cots late at night, smoking cigarettes. They're talking about the first three things they'll do on the day they get out of jail. Write their conversation.

ᴐ Create a mood simply by describing a room. Make it cheerful; depressing; scary; poignant.

ᴐ Use these three words in a short paragraph: baseball, poetry, fortune cookie.

ᴐ my mother's boyfriend

ᴐ A very old woman, in her nineties, is taken out to lunch by her teenage grandchildren. She tells them something surprising. What is it, and how does it change their relationship?

ᴐ bare winter trees, looking like _____

ᴐ _____ sunrise

ᴐ the _____ sound of the twigs breaking

ᴐ the fragile _____ of hope

ᴐ the _____ of sailors

 ◡ _____ *by sun*

 ◡ *Describe someone praying.*

 ◡ *various kinds of behaviors in a movie theater*

 ◡ *how to enjoy spring*

 ◡ *Someone has a dream that makes her/him change her/his mind about something. What is the dream? What action gets taken as a result of it?*

 ◡ *You and your mother are waiting in the emergency room for news of your father, who has had a heart attack. When the doctor comes out, it is clear from the look on his face that he has news for you. What does the doctor say, how does he look saying it, and what are the reactions that follow?*

∾ ∾ ∾

 ◡ *If your bed could talk, how would it describe you?*

 ◡ *You overhear someone confessing his or her sins. What you hear makes you want to laugh. What is it that you hear? Now imagine that what you hear makes you want to cry; makes you furious.*

 ◡ *the best/worst advice you ever got*

ᴗ If, when you were a kid, you'd been give one hundred dollars, what would you have bought? If you were given a thousand dollars now, what would you do with it?

ᴗ the best kind of candy and why

ᴗ Describe a first day of school; a last day.

ᴗ Name fifteen things you see in a garden.

ᴗ Using first person, describe what a mother feels upon hearing her baby's first cry. Now, again using first person, describe what a father feels. Now be the baby.

ᴗ Your father tells you for the first time about the day your older sister, whom you never knew, died. Write not only what he says, but also what he does with his coffee cup as he tells you.

ᴗ Quite unexpectedly, you get called up onto a stage to perform with a band. You can't sing or play any instrument. What do you do instead?

ᴗ You are a guest at a good friend's wedding. When you enter the church, you are told that the bride wants to see you. When you come into the room where she is, she is standing with her back to you. When she turns around, you are surprised. Why? What do you do?

ও *Describe a picnic in a cemetery.*

ও *as likely as a trip to* _____

ও *angry* _____ *s,* _____ *ing*

ও *light as a* _____

ও *the* _____ *of envy in my*

ও _____ *glow*

⌒⌒ ⌒⌒ ⌒⌒

ও *A very shy girl, one who means a lot to you, is starting college. She asks you for a phrase she can use as a mantra, to give herself courage and comfort. What do you tell her?*

ও *An old friend of yours has never been able to talk to you about her deceased parents. Finally, one day she opens up. She tells you they were killed in an accident that always makes people laugh, even though they want very much not to. Describe the accident.*

ও *Use these three words in a short paragraph: magazine, pantry, telephone.*

ᴖ *You are allowed to relive one day or experience from the time you were thirteen. What do you choose? Now be your mother, doing the same thing; now your father; now your grandmother; now your grandfather.*

ᴖ *the* _____ *end of the journey*

ᴖ *tiny as* _____

ᴖ *newborn's hands, shaped like* _____

ᴖ _____ *icicles*

ᴖ *proud* _____

ᴖ *the visceral pull of* _____

ᴖ *the carnival smell of* _____

ᴖ *demure* _____ *, dressed in*

ᴖ *that* _____ *y smell of summer*

ᴖ *You are a fourteen-year-old, told to make a will. What do you leave to whom?*

ᴖ *a vivid memory of something that occurred on a school bus* ɯ List five different colors that describe the sky. Now list five different moods that do the same.

ɯ You are a nurse, told to collect a urine sample from someone who does not speak English. How do you communicate what you need? How does the person respond?

ᖆᕵ ᖆᕵ ᖆᕵ

ɯ Use these three words in a paragraph: gum, beard, truck.

ɯ Your significant other has planned a trip that he/she "knows" you'll really love. Every waking hour has been planned. Describe the trip in detail, as though you were telling your best friend about it, and do it in two ways: First, as though you really will love it; then, as though your honey has you figured all wrong, and you will hate it.

ɯ the cruelest thing you ever saw

ɯ the cruelest thing you ever did

ɯ What taught me about pride was _____.

ɯ He slumped down in his chair, and everything about the way he looked could be summed up in one word:

_____.

○ *You find an old jewelry box at the back of a closet. In it is a feather, a diamond bracelet wrapped in a scrap of black velvet, and a note. Describe the feather and the bracelet. Who is the note to? What does it say?*

○ *Provide one line of dialogue as a response to these questions:*

> *How did you know it was love?*

> *What does swimming feel like?*

> *What could you never forgive?*

> *Why do people need to believe in God?*

○ *Describe five completely different types of people placing their order for coffee with the same waitress. Describe these people in appearance, movement, and speech. If you like, also describe the waitress's reaction to them.*

∞ ∞ ∞

○ *If you are a man, write about how it feels to have an abortion. If you are a woman, write about how it feels to be a man in the waiting room while your woman has an abortion.*

ꙮ *sadness feeling like a* _____ *in the chest*

ꙮ *flat green of a* _____

ꙮ *the* _____ *of the praying mantis*

ꙮ *the* _____ *of fall*

ꙮ *settled over my shoulders like* _____

ꙮ *a line of pain like* _____

ꙮ *an anger so fierce I could feel it in my* _____

ꙮ Use these three words in a sentence or short paragraph: kneel, heat, wooden door.

ꙮ Room by room, describe your ideal house.

ꙮ Give a guided tour of a mouse's house.

ꙮ What about you embarrassed your kids?

ꙮ What about your parents embarrasses you?

ꙮ Write a description of something you look at every day in three different types of light (e.g., morning sun, dusk, lamplight).

⌣ Set a timer for two minutes, during which time you look carefully at your thumb. When the timer goes off, write about what you saw. Describe not only the anatomy of that part of your body, but also what it suggests to you: the wonder of what a thumb does; memories it brings back; fantasies (if I lost my thumbs . . . if dogs had thumbs . . . if a piano piece were written to be played with only thumbs . . .).

∾ ∾ ∾

⌣ In a small box, collect things with various textures: stones, twigs, fabric swatches, feathers, etc. From time to time, write a detailed description of how a few of them feel.

⌣ why she/he was such a good kisser

⌣ a brush with death

⌣ an encounter between a woman and a door-to-door salesman, in 1948

⌣ how men wrap presents versus how women wrap presents

⌣ As a kid, I thought soul food was _____.

ᴗ *In your dream, you are talking face-to-face with God.*
  He looks like _____.

ᴗ *your favorite cup*

∾ ∾ ∾

Homework

Make up ten of your own exercises.

> Place is one of the lesser angels—feeling wears
> the crown.
>
> —EUDORA WELTY

Passion is everywhere: in love, in religion and politics, in cooking and gardening, in learning, in art, in devotion to one's family, in solitude and the search for self. But if I had to come up with one word to describe what *writing* passionately is all about, the word would be "risk." Because that's what emotionally intense communication requires: You must be willing (and courageous enough) to show others the most private parts of yourself, holding back nothing. But first you must be willing to show those parts to *yourself*, to acknowledge in a conscious way their presence in you.

If you are willing—perhaps even eager—to more fully access your passion in order to put it into your writing, there are some things it may be helpful to think about. Write out your response to the following in your journal:

- What does the word "passion" mean or imply to you?
- Where in your body does passion reside?
- Using body parts and/or functions only, describe how it feels to be sexually stimulated; angry; sad; frightened; moved; determined; shocked; restless.

- Now, understanding that passion is often a mixture of emotions, describe having two or more of the above feelings at the same time.
- What are some of the different ways passion makes you behave? How do you feel about yourself or someone else acting that way?
- What is passion's worth? What is its danger?
- When you read passionate writing of any kind, do you enjoy it, or does it make you feel uncomfortable? Why?
- Without looking at it again, recall the last great love scene you read or saw—or imagined. List as many peripheral elements that were involved as you can remember (consider, for example, the clothing, the background noises, the light). Now recall a scene involving great anger, despair, or fear. What elements were involved in each of them?

I believe in order to write passionately, you need to catch fire. You need to get carried along by something that's stronger—and wilder and braver and perhaps truer—than your normal self. You need to send your superego out to run some errands and then let yourself go: Be mindless of others' conventions or opinions—even your own—and of consequence, too. You need to behave as you do when you're in the middle of great sex: You have to be blind and yet see extraordinarily clearly at the same time; you have to feel very nearly unstoppable.

So. How do you put that kind of passion in your writing? Here's one way to start:

As a nurse, I once helped teach a sex-education class to a group of high school seniors. The first night the class met, my co-instructor and I hung huge sheets of white paper along the walls, with one word printed at the top of each page. There were words that were the names of body parts, like *penis* and *vagina*; there were charged words, like *intercourse* and *masturbation*; and there were more seemingly innocuous words like *man, woman,* and *date.* We gave the students magic markers and told them we wanted them to list synonyms for each word, as well as any other words or phrases that came to mind. We asked that they try to have no inhibitions; that there was, for this exercise at least, no unacceptable language. Then we left the room for a while.

When we came back, we saw what you might expect: a long list of words on each page, in handwriting ranging from tightly small to bold. Many of the words would have been shocking under other circumstances. But what happened during this exercise was that the students did more than giggle at their sanctioned naughtiness: They learned things. They discovered how utterly silly some of the language is (as well as how damaging it can be); and they took a giant step toward being comfortable with and talking freely about the kinds of things we were going to discuss. When all of us said the list of words out loud together, barriers were broken down. That's because once you've said the worst word imaginable for one thing or another, it's much easier to say something lower down on the Richter scale.

What I would like to encourage you to do in this chapter is to break down your own barriers, to go to your own outer limits—and then beyond. One reason to do that is to learn the same thing those students did: ease in handling things that might previously have been uncomfortable or taboo. Another reason is to try to learn some deeper truths about emotions: what they're really like; how many things they involve; how you can best show that in words. So much writing about deep feeling takes the form of cliché, but it never has to.

It's possible that a few of the things I suggest will require your visiting your dark side, something many of us don't like to do. But if you want to write from a place of emotional integrity, it's important to learn everything you can about all kinds of emotions, including those that exist in you, that you wish didn't.

That is not to say that this chapter should be a primer in writing pornography or violence. It is only to say that human feeling is deep and complex and full of variety; and anyone who wants to can find it worth exploring, both in themselves and in others.

To get at emotion, both in yourself and in your writing, you have to start with feelings. Some of our feelings originate mysteriously and reside in us in the same way; but many more come overtly and directly from that most wonderful (and portable) of gifts—our senses. The more we utilize them, the more attention we pay to the excellent information they provide us, the richer our writing can be.

Seeing
It is not enough to give a passing glance to something if you want to really see it. Whether you are talking about the

colors of an island sunset or the grime in a down-and-outer's flophouse bathroom, you have to look deeply. You have to give yourself enough time to transcend the impulse we usually have of naming or classifying something—thereby often dismissing it. To really see something is to let yourself move beyond the narrow place of words and into a 360-degree kind of noticing, an act which, if done correctly, temporarily takes up all of a person, and utilizes much more than the eyes—utilizes, for example, the heart and the soul.

Seeing deeply requires a kind of telescoping vision: looking at the surface of something and then beyond that, and then beyond that. Oftentimes this requires only that you let your eyes look longer than they might ordinarily. Other times it means you look not only at but into, or that you move something aside in order to look behind, or under, or through.

One way to describe things that you see in an interesting way is to be aware of what something reminds you of. Some of the most charming and effective descriptions I've read are those that let me see a familiar thing newly. This kind of prose is akin to poetry; it utilizes the power of metaphor. For example, I remember my then-three-year-old daughter seeing snow that had been dirtied by trucks spewing out tan-colored sand. She said, "The snow looks like crumb cake," and she was exactly right. But it took her telling me that to see it. You want to solicit in your readers that same pleasant rush of recognition, that satisfying surprise of finding out something they knew but didn't know they knew.

When you're looking at something, be aware of substructure—look not only at a face, but the bones beneath it. Notice subtleties and gradations in the color and form of everything, and focus especially on the details of what you see. Those details tell the real story, and make you see things in the most concrete way. Consider, for example, poet and gardening enthusiast Celia Thaxter's 1894 description of a poppy:

> It is held upright upon a straight and polished stem, its petals curving upward and outward into the cup of light, pure gold with a lustrous satin sheen; a rich orange is painted on the gold, drawn in infinitely fine lines to a point in the center of the edge of each petal, so that the effect is that of a diamond of flame in a cup of gold.

After reading that description, who could ever look at a poppy in the same way? This author not only tells us what she sees, she makes us see it, too. And this is a gift that gives in two directions: The reader is enriched by being able to see something that he may not have seen before; and the writer is enriched because of the connection she makes.

Whether you're writing fiction or nonfiction, you can greatly help define a character by sharing not only what he says and does, but also how he looks. Again, details matter. Don't tell the reader that someone is old; show it by describing the dime-size age spots, the sag of the cheeks, the see-through hair, the spiderlike spread of veins at the back of the knees. Are nylons falling down? Are belts too big? Are there greasy thumbprints on the lenses of the bifocals? Is the posture stooped or stubbornly erect? Is there a periodic squeal from a hearing aid? What does he eat for breakfast? How does she speak on the phone? Do medication bottles rattle in his front pocket? Does she keep nitro-glycerin in a silver monogrammed case?

You can also define your characters by showing how *they* see; you can in that way differentiate between levels of sensitivity. I know a woman who said she couldn't stand to be with her boyfriend anymore when he found utterly uninspiring a display of artwork that moved her to tears. How would you write *that* scene?

Hearing

When you want to listen to any sound, be it a human voice or the buzz of a bee, you must afford it respectful attention. You have to be fully present and not distracted by what you *think* about what you're hearing. To do that, you need to move beyond your ears; to hear things not only in your head, but also in your center. That is to say, not only hear sound, *feel* it.

When you are listening to language, don't attend only to the meaning of the words being spoken. Hear how those words are said, feel the emotions behind them, see the gestures—both broad and minute—that accompany them. Hear, too, the absence of sound: when and where it occurs, what that implies. Notice how silence can be more powerful than words, how it can communicate a wealth of emotion, both positive and negative.

Careful listening without pen in hand is the first step in learning to write believable dialogue. Pay attention to the way people really talk. Notice everything. What are the different speeds and rhythms and levels of volume that you hear in speech? Is the phrasing so lyrical as to be musical or so flat as to be a monotone? What varieties are there in accents? How can someone's attitude toward life in general be conveyed by what he says in a few sentences, and how he says it? What kind of breathing occurs between sentences? How and why do people stutter and stammer, hem and haw? What is the difference between a name being said as a caress versus a reprimand?

A good description of ambient sound can help readers visualize a place, thus making them better able to put themselves into the scene you're creating. If, for example, you were writing a scene that took place in an airport, what sounds would make it seem more real? How about a hair salon? A funeral parlor? A kitchen? A bar?

Sound can fine-tune the description of a place, too. Consider what you might hear at 7:30 in the evening at these three places, all of them restaurants: a four-star hotel dining room, a truck stop, a Dairy Queen on a hot summer night.

The mood of a scene, too, can be created or greatly enhanced by sound. What do these things suggest: a grandfather clock ticking; a dog howling; the keys of a computer clacking; thunder booming; birds singing; a train whistle fading away; the rattle of a window in winter wind; one finger tapping on a tabletop; a cigarette being ground out in a metal ashtray; a child softly singing; a woman sobbing; a radio station being changed, then changed again, then changed again; a door slamming versus a door being slowly creaked open.

Consider, too, the myriad reactions we have to sound. What strong feelings can be called up by what we hear? Nostalgia? Fear? Loss? Lust? Sadness? Joy? Bravado?

Tasting

One of the reasons babies put everything in their mouths is that they haven't yet learned it's a socially unacceptable way to find out about something. But you can understand the inclination: The tongue is a very earnest and talented explorer. You can find out a lot from putting various things in your mouth, be it a No. 2 pencil, a fireball piece of candy, or your lover's earlobe. Pay attention. When you taste something, go beyond a single sensation: Try to be aware of the many components present, which we limit by describing with only one word.

The sensation of taste can quite successfully transmigrate. "Sweet," for example, can describe not only a Godiva chocolate, but also a certain kind of kiss or an old, familiar movement—or moment. "Sour" can apply to a relationship gone wrong or an unpleasant disposition.

There is a great deal of pleasure associated with taste, and this can be wonderfully well represented in what you write. Think not only of the satisfaction found in tasting food, of course. Consider things like the salty pleasure found in the pocket of the elbow, the blank sweetness of wax, the clean green taste at the white end of a weed.

The mechanics of tasting yield an amazing variety of method and effect. Notice what you do with your mouth when you eat a caramel versus a potato chip versus a spoonful of soup. What are the movements that occur when you kiss your lover, let ice cream melt on your tongue, tear into an Italian sub?

Can you think of how richly a person's character can be defined by how—or what—he chews? When I was a little girl, a man who once ate dinner at our house chewed so wildly open-mouthed (and otherwise had such appalling table manners) that he literally nauseated my mother. (Of course, he thrilled us kids.)

On the other hand, I once knew a woman who made eating ice cubes seem comparable to dining at Le Cirque. She did it only in the summer, sitting outside in the backyard in a chaise lounge, wearing shorts and a halter top, and pin curls in her hair. She painted her toenails, smoked and read magazines, and chewed ice cubes that dropped one by one from a magenta-colored aluminum tumbler into her heavily lipsticked mouth, and I have yet to see anyone make anything look more delicious.

How do the images of these two people compare or contrast to that of a bowlegged cowboy scooping up beans from a tin plate? Or an old woman sitting alone at her tiny kitchen table gumming a chicken leg to death?

You can use taste to describe fear, but please, please, *please* do not use, "the metallic taste of fear," even though fear *does* taste metallic. Think of what *else* it tastes like, or describe fear another way. If one more person uses that overworked metaphor, all writers will be struck dead by the god of vocabulary.

You can conjure up nostalgia by describing the taste of a Thanksgiving dinner, or Aunt Sylvia's matzoh balls, or a hot dog at the ballpark on a day when you sat knee to knee with your hero dad. You can use taste to provide humor to a scene, too: Have your characters savor very unusual things; or common things at uncommon times. (Imagine a scene where one character might say to another, "Do you have to eat that *now?*")

You can show an indecisive person trying to decide what to eat, tasting every single thing in the refrigerator, including the baking soda. You can also bring levity to an otherwise sorrowful scene: A heartbroken woman sits at the kitchen table in her bathrobe, regularly interrupting her pathetic crying jag by taking huge bites from a Dutch oven full of mashed potatoes and butter.

Touching

What amazing variety is at our disposal when we want to gather information from this most sensuous of senses! Think: the petals of a rose, the surface of a desk, the underbelly of a kitten, the skin of a snake, the bark of a tree. Mud. Cactus. The edges of endive. Cold cream. The sharp end of a straight pin.

And what a wide range of responses we can have to someone touching *us*: an eager alertness, teeth-clenching irritability, a comfortable leaning into, a fearful pulling back.

Think of how touch works. Where does an impulse come from? Where does it go, and in what ways does it manifest itself? How does it feel to become deeply aware of touch? What is the difference, say, in absentmindedly touching the valley at the base of your neck when you're watching television or talking on the phone versus lying alone in a dark room, concentrating on nothing but that?

Sometimes touch in writing can be so dramatic, it is best for you to *under*play it. Someone I know once wrote about his father beating him with a board when he was a small child. The horror of that act is in the act itself; it would suffer from embellishment. But to describe a good kiss requires more than your saying "It was a good kiss." A reader wants to know *why* it was a good kiss, how it felt; he or she wants to feel it, too.

Often, as in other senses, there are conflicting emotions in touch: Consider a woman who is not encouraged to socialize with other men at a party; her husband keeps his arm around her, but it feels less like affection than a leash. Or imagine a man who is cruelly belittled by his lover, then given a kiss. What would that kiss feel like? What mixed feelings are in the embrace of a mother saying good-bye to her college-bound firstborn?

Touch can say so much in writing, with such economy. It can be one of the best tools at your disposal for showing personality in an indirect way. Have your characters communicate with touch in addition to language, but try to avoid clichés here as well. Look for the unusual, for the not so obvious. Watch people and the way they touch themselves and each other: There really is a language of the body. Notice how the face may be saying one thing, but the hands another, as when someone is smiling with fists clenched so tightly their knuckles are white. Be aware of subtlety: A person who is nervous doesn't usually emulate the ever tremulous Don Knotts; that emotion more often shows itself in the tiniest of ways: a finger to the eyebrow— twice. A too quick smile. The placement of the pocketbook in the exact center of the lap. A show of red at the top of the ears. The quietest of throat clearings.

To best use touch in your writing, heighten your own awareness. You can build up sensory ability in the same way that you can build up your body—"exercise" both the part of you that allows you to differentiate between cactus and velvet as well as the part of you that makes you respond with everything from adoration to disdain. It doesn't have to be difficult or complicated to do this. For example, one of my favorite gifts is a box of fabric swatches that a friend gave me. Inside the box are pieces of leather, suede, velvet, silk, cotton, and more. On top of the box is one word: *touch*. And I do, both for the pleasure and the practice.

As for "exercising" your responses, sharing them openly and more fully—and with more people—ought to help a lot.

Smelling

One of the reasons old people lose their appetite is that they lose their sense of smell. One of the reasons the perfume industry makes so much money is because of our Pied Piper–like response to an alluring scent. One of the reasons given for the phenomenon of falling in love is pheromones.

So smell is very important. It is also probably the most underutilized of all the senses in writing. But in the same way that a movie in "real life" is enhanced by the smell of popcorn, a written scene about a hospital is enhanced by describing the antiseptic smell. As an ocean scene is enhanced by evoking a saltwater smell. As a scene of going home is enhanced by including the smell of meatloaf coming from your mother's oven.

Don't overuse smell in your writing—as in life, a little goes a long way. But don't overlook it, either. And remember to look for new ways of describing things: What does bread smell like *besides* yeasty?

Don't be afraid to try more creative ways of using smell, either. Can the scent of a perfume be described by a color? Can a certain odor best be described by an emotion, as in "the defeating smell of the subway" or "the stuck-up smell of the first-class lounge"? How about "the musky leftovers of an afternoon of pleasure" or "the acrid evidence of fear"?

By taking advantage of all that your senses offer, you'll become a much more interesting and versatile writer. You'll be able to move past superficial and predictable writing and into the kind of description that evokes real feeling in your readers. Your own passion will be felt by them. You'll connect.

Exercises

1. *In your journal, describe the following things as thoroughly as you can: a painting by a Dutch master; the words spoken (and the way they are spoken) by someone who is very frightened; the difference between the tastes of a pickle, fried chicken, and chocolate cake; the feel of a feather; the smell of a stick of cinnamon gum.*

2. *(This is the only exercise I want you to do outside your journal, because I want you to burn it when it's done. This is so you'll feel really free to write anything.)*
    Using first person, present tense, write these scenes, making them full of passion:

ഄ *You having sex with someone of the opposite sex;*
   with someone of the same sex; with yourself.

ഄ *Two scenes wherein you kill someone—one where*
   the murder could be seen as justified, one where it
   could not.

ഄ *Write a hate letter; write a love letter from someone*
   who doesn't have a chance with the object of his/her
   desire.

ഄ *Make a terrible confession.*

3. *Now write a scene that will show you your own ability*
   to accelerate and decelerate: Create two people who
   are obviously very much in love, and put them
   anywhere. Write them having a conversation that
   turns into a vicious argument. Make the argument get
   worse and worse, the voices louder and louder, the
   physical gestures bigger and more threatening. Now
   take the characters back down the emotional scale, to
   a place of reconciliation and even greater affection.

When you are writing, your characters will do anything
you tell them to. Your job is to make sure that what they do
and say feels *earned.* You want their speech and actions to
make sense, so that a reader will feel she can follow a story
along in a kind of seamless, dreamy way, believing every
word. Otherwise, you can bet she will in one way or
another pull away from the book. (She might even be like a

friend of mine who, when she feels a book rings false, throws it across the room.)

One of the most important things I can tell you about writing is that you should always strive for authenticity, both with your characters as well as in your writing in general. To do that, it helps to know as much as you can about feelings—your own and those of others. Have the courage to open your eyes and your heart, and to go deep, and then deeper. Look for the moment and the way that people really reveal themselves, and be receptive to that. Learn to find and accept the weak spots in yourself and in others: That's where the tenderness—and the truth—lie.

Homework

Look again at the work you did for the homework assignment at the end of "In Your Own Words." Now rewrite that piece, this time infusing it with much more feeling. Then take a bubble bath, put on a silk robe, and eat some bonbons. Even if you're a guy.

6 *The Good Liar: Making the Move from Nonfiction to Fiction*

Art is a lie that makes us realize the truth.
—PICASSO

When I first began publishing, I had no interest in writing fiction. That's because I didn't think I *could*. It seemed impossible to me, the notion of making so many things up, then making it all seem believable besides.

But there came a time when I wanted to try fiction anyway—something yanked at my sleeve; I wanted to do more than I had been doing, to go off in a new direction. So one day I sat down and nervously wrote a short story featuring a woman in love with a man she shouldn't have been in love with. I felt very, very uncomfortable doing this; not because the story was terrible, or because it was hard to write fiction (though both those things were true), but because I was putting things on the page that had never happened as though they had. I felt as though I might be arrested by fact checkers.

When I brought my story to my writing group, however, they were completely comfortable with what I had done. They talked about my characters as though they were real people—which actually made for a kind of pleasant embarrassment. They treated the situation I created as something that really could have happened. Thus was born my career as a professional liar, a.k.a. fiction writer.

I think a lot of people who want to write fiction shy away from it because they think of it as being radically different from nonfiction. It is different; but it is also very much *like* writing nonfiction.

For one thing, no matter what you're writing, if you want others to read it, it must be interesting. People who appear on the page need to be fleshed out, so that they don't seem like "cardboard" characters. Dialogue must emulate the way people really talk. Descriptions should help make a scene feel real; they should enrich and advance the story. Perhaps most important, a piece of writing has to "go somewhere"; a reader needs to feel as though there's a good reason she's put aside all else in order to pay attention to you. It might be in the hope of having an epiphany; it might be to resonate, or to wax nostalgic; it might be to learn; it might be to laugh; it might be to live vicariously; it might be simply to revel in the beauty of the language; but there has to be a *reason* to read something.

In that respect, writing fiction is simply using the same skills and care you use in writing nonfiction, but to write about something that did not happen, that is not true. Not true in the literal sense, anyway. But fiction has to be *emotionally* true. In fact, I have found that, in many ways, fiction is "truer" than nonfiction; there's something about the form that can make you tell the larger truths. Perhaps it's because when you are making up a story, you are offered some sort of protection. It is not you, out there, alone; it is you, behind something.

For me, the biggest difference between nonfiction and fiction has to do with the way I feel writing it—the contrast between feeling grounded versus that of having a waking dream. Writing nonfiction is like a three-in-the-afternoon, sunny-day walk, where one foot naturally precedes the other toward a known destination, where the path both behind and ahead is well defined. Writing fiction, on the other hand, feels like being in some dark place where I don't see anything well, but I walk on anyway, trusting in something I cannot really define, having no idea where I'll end up. I may start with certain grounding facts as an impetus or inspiration, but I end up changing them pretty radically in the process of liftoff. As I go on, other "facts" become woven into the story in a way that feels more like chance than design. (And in the process of shaping those facts to fit in the story, they often become changed, too.)

I believe that fiction feeds on itself, grows like a pregnancy. The more you write, the more there is to draw from; the more you say, the more there *is* to say. The deeper you go into your imagination, the richer that reservoir becomes. You do not run out of material by using all that's in you; rather, when you take everything that is available one day, it only makes room for new things to appear the next.

There is a certain degree of faith required in writing fiction. I can tell you with certainty that if you feel a strong urge to do it, the "how" of it will come. You don't need to know a whole book in order to write the first page. You don't even need to know the end of the first page. You need only the desire to create something that will say what you feel needs to be said, however vague its form at the beginning. You need a willingness to discover the wealth and wisdom of your own subconscious, and to trust that it will tell you what to do and how to do it—not all at once, but as needed, step by step. You have to take a deep breath, let go of your usual control, and then begin walking in the dark.

MATERIAL

Whenever people ask me where I get my material, I am genuinely befuddled. "Well . . . from *life!*" is what I usually say. What I mean is that each of us, no matter who we are or what we do, is offered potential story ideas daily. The people we know, the things that happen to them and us, the random scenes we witness and the conversations we overhear—all of these things are rich with raw material; all of them are capable of serving as a vehicle or springboard for a good story, in one way or another. We need only be aware. We need only be awake, and curious, and willing to share. (In fact, I would say those last three are the only things you *really* need to write *any*thing—fiction or not.)

To be more specific: Think of all that is at the buffet table for your consideration each day: the sight of hair in sunshine, a small kindness from one stranger on the street to another, a grave injustice on a playground, the feel of veins on a leaf, the swell of anger in your own throat. Think of the inadvertent charm and humor you can find in people everywhere. Once, sitting at a baseball game, I heard someone say, "Well, I'll tell you *what*. I'll tell you WHAT!! . . . That's all I'm going to say." Another time, at a bar, I heard a long-legged man drawl sympathetically to his friend, "Yeeuuup. *That'll* challenge your nerves!" From those two lines alone, you could take a stab at creating two distinct characters— and it's likely you'd succeed.

To find your stories, look closely at your job and the people you work with, at your family and the changing dynamics therein, at human-interest pieces in the newspapers. Read the advice columns—if you want some real *character* characters, that's a great place to find them. Look for a message in a painting, in a photograph, in the dirty rainbow of an oil-tainted puddle. Look to your heart—to its soaring and its grieving; look to your many moods, your vulnerabilities, your learning and changing, your strongest beliefs, your deepest fears, your triumphs and failures.

Ultimately, for me, and I think for you, too, it is not so much a problem of finding material as it is limiting it, deciding what should stay in. (And of course there is the problem of how best to shape that material into a good *story*, but that "problem" is also the pleasure in writing fiction.)

Don't feel you need to write something "different" every time you write a piece of fiction. If you want to, that's fine. But I have come to see that many writers write about the same thing over and over—not specifically, of course, but generally. For example, I am interested in love and relationships and women's issues, and I seem to focus on that in every novel I write, whether I intend to or not. And in the same way that I like people walking around in robes and curlers, I like the small human dramas that get played out in kitchens rather than in exotic locales. I rarely mention place at all in the books I write, because where my characters live is beside the point; the only topography that concerns me is interior. That's not to say that I don't greatly admire writers who *are* concerned with place. But I think you need to come to terms with what *your* real passions are; and then realize they will show up again and again in what you write. And that's fine.

As a line of dialogue can help form a character, it can also be the germ of an entire novel. So can one random scene you witness. So can a feeling about something you read. Look over the writing exercises you did for Chapter 5. Aren't there possibilities everywhere for something much bigger than you might have thought?

VOICE

Voice is most simply defined as the way you tell a story, your style. It is not necessarily the way you talk, although it can be. Rather it is the personality beneath the words, the current that runs through a story, the thing the reader must be able to believe in, and trust. She must also like the voice. That's not to say that she must like the character— the character can be a mass murderer, after all.

James Joyce said, "All fiction is fantasized autobiography." I believe that, too, in the sense that when you are writing fiction, you have to *become* the story's teller. You have to assume that person's point of view, know as much as you can what he or she feels—not only about the things you are writing about, but about everything else, as well. You also must stay in character. It's the same in a book as it is on the stage: If you fall out of character, you undermine your authority and the authenticity of your story; and it is entirely likely that you will lose your audience's interest.

There is a voice that is more natural for you than others, one that works better than anything else. You may already write in your own voice; it may be something you "came with" and never give a second thought to, something so inherent you are hard-pressed to define it or think of it as separate from yourself. Or you may need to work hard at discovering your voice.

One way you might be able to do this is by writing the same paragraph in a number of different styles, noticing what feels best—and most honest—to you. (It will also feel the easiest.) Once you've discovered your voice, you will see it develop more with each thing you write, and you will have more confidence about the way to approach anything you try.

I believe the most important thing about voice is to *respect your own*. Do not try to sound like someone else, however much you may admire him or her. It's unfair to you, to the person you're trying to copy, and to the reader. And it probably won't work, anyway.

MOOD

In fiction as in nonfiction, mood is all in the details. It's far more effective to describe a peeling ceiling, cockroaches running from the light, and a toilet bowl orange with rust stains than to say "His apartment was depressing." Similarly, to say "She felt happy" is to massively gyp the reader. In what way did she feel happy? How did her face look? What did she feel inside her chest? Trust your imagination to supply you with such details, and don't be afraid to try anything. Remember, you are the one in charge—you can change or eliminate anything you don't like later.

When you are creating a mood in nonfiction, you have available your memories of a real place or event, and you can pick and choose among all the details you actually observed—lighting, sounds, smells, voices, clothing, etc.— to help re-create the scene. It can be a bit overwhelming to think of having to create all those things yourself, to pick and choose from myriad possibilities to find the one specific thing that will work best. But remember that the whole picture need not come into focus at once. Concentrate on getting to know your character and write with feeling about him or her; other details will come as a natural by-product.

You can create a certain artful synergy by showing how someone feels on the inside and then setting up a kind of echo in the physical surroundings. Don't *over*do this, though: Don't have someone whose heart is breaking standing before the window watching the driving rain and then see some old geezer get beat up on the street—the rain is enough. Consider too how effective contrast can be—if that same heartbroken person stands before her window looking out on to a perfectly beautiful day, it can make her anguish seem even worse.

DIALOGUE

When I write dialogue, I feel as though I'm merely the typist, transcribing what the characters say inside my head. I don't have the sense that I'm making anything up. I "hear" the conversations I write as clearly as those I hear when I eavesdrop on people in a café. Sometimes it's hard for me to keep up with a conversation my characters are having; typically, a first draft of dialogue is full of typos.

I have always found writing dialogue easy. I believe part of the reason for that is that I love to listen to the way people talk, and have therefore been "studying" dialogue all my life. Another reason is that I don't plan what my characters will say any more than I plan what I'm going to say in real life. Conversations evolve before me, with one line of dialogue leading naturally into the next.

Of course, in order to do this, you have to really know your characters. They need to have distinct personalities that are reflected by what they say. The reader—and you—have to be able to tell the difference between your characters based solely on the way they speak: Lines of dialogue should not be interchangeable among them, at least not when they are speaking from the heart about something that matters to them.

Try this: In your journal, write out as much as you can recall of an interesting conversation you recently had with someone you know very well. Then, make up a conversation between the two of you.

Now make up two people who are opposites, different as they can be. Side by side, list characteristics of each personality. Make the list as long and as detailed as you can. Think for a while about who those people are, without writing anything—go for a walk and think about them, if you can. Then write out a conversation between the two of them, about the same thing you and your friend talked about.

What your characters say should reflect not only the

specificity of their unique personalities, but general human nature as well. For example, oftentimes people hide what they really want to say by saying something else entirely. Or they whisper when they want to shout. Or they intentionally de-emphasize something they care very deeply about. Your job as a writer is to make sure the reader knows what your characters *mean*, despite what they say.

Finally, there is a certain rhythm in spoken language as opposed to written, a recognizable quality that might best be described as improvisational. One of the most common problems in poor dialogue is that it simply doesn't sound the way people really talk. Read your dialogue aloud, preferably into a tape recorder. Could you mistake what you hear for a real conversation? Are there pauses and/or hesitancies? ("I said I'd tell you. I said I would. So . . . fine. Here goes.") Are there corrections? ("We had six—no, wait—*seven* beers!") Did you use idioms like "I mean" and "you know"? How about elipses? (And then it was just . . . it was done.") Perhaps most important, is emotion represented? Can a reader see how the character feels, saying what he does?

When you write dialogue, you do not need to identify a speaker every time he or she speaks. This is something that's very common when people first start to write dialogue, and it's a hard habit to break. You feel rather insecure not saying who's talking. But believe me, you can do without most of your "he said" and "she said." Try this: Write a page of a story with lots of dialogue, and do not identify any speaker. Then go back and put in a reference only when a reader *really wouldn't know* who a speaker is.

There are times when you'll use a "he/she said" not for

purposes of identification, but because you want the rhythm, the pacing, that comes from adding that phrase. Or you'll use it because you want to force a brief pause that the reader would not otherwise take. But that should happen rarely. In a typical back-and-forth conversation between two people, you need to identify the speakers only once. If it is a very long conversation, you might want to throw in a reminder to the reader as to who is talking, but not too often. Remember, too, that identifying a speaker can be done by something other than "he said/she said" as in "'I don't care.' Randy stood up, his face flushed, and dropped the priceless china cup and saucer to the floor. 'There. How do you like that?'"

Be wary of using words like "snarled" or "shouted" or "purred" in writing dialogue. Your reader should almost always be able to tell how something is said by the words that are used and the scene in which they occur. The same holds true with adverbs. If your character is saying "I hate you!" it's completely unnecessary to add "he said angrily." (And if it's being said playfully, that should be evident without the adverb, too.)

CONJURING REALISTIC CHARACTERS

E. M. Forster said, "We all like to pretend we don't use real people, but one does actually." I think this is true, but only to a certain extent. When you first start to write fiction, you may draw heavily from people you know. But as you go on, you will probably find your characters only vaguely inspired by acquaintances.

For example, in the novel I am working on now, the narrator begins the book by saying, "You know people like me. I'm the one who sat on a folding chair out in the hall with a cigar box on my lap, selling tickets to the prom, but never going to one." Did I actually know someone like that? Not really. It is more a case of having been aware that there were people like that in my high school, as I suppose there were (and continue to be) in every high school. What I want to do in writing this book is move behind this character's eyes, to become her as much as I can. I want to see the world from her point of view, to tell what she sees and how that feels. The character she is specifically comes from general ideas I have about how people like her might feel.

Which leads me to an important point. As far as I'm concerned, the most important thing you need when inventing characters is empathy. You have to have some ability to really put yourself in others' shoes, to feel as much as you can what they feel. The more successful you are at doing this, the more realistic your characters are.

There must have been many people you've met about whom you've idly—or actively—wondered. Maybe it was someone you worked with who was incredibly quiet, just came and did her job, then went home, never saying anything more than she had to to anyone. Someone like that might move you to think, *What's her life like away from here? Does she ever date? Is her apartment incredibly neat? Does she talk to her mom every weekend? Does she sit at some little desk and write incredibly erotic poetry that she'll never show to anyone?* Think of the homeless people on the street to whom you give change. When you look into their eyes, what do you see there? Who are they? Who were they?

When you write a character, you have an opportunity to see another way. I think it's always good to have a certain kind of respect for the characters you draw—to try to present their side of things with some integrity, whether they are "good" people or not. It's also important to remember that no one is all black or all white; it's the mix of positive and negative qualities in us that makes us real, that makes us human (and interesting!); and it's that same mix that will make someone you create believable. Nothing undermines a character more than making him too good or too bad: If he's too bad, your reader will lose faith in you as the writer; if he's too good, your reader may want to upchuck.

You need not always look outside yourself for characters. You have many different sides to yourself. All of those sides can be used to help create realistic personalities. For example, it's not that hard to write about someone who's lonely all the time when you've been lonely sometimes. Similarly, if you've ever been angry to the point of irrationality, you can draw on those feelings to help make up some sort of lunatic. There is enough inside you to help create or enhance almost any kind of character—as in method acting, enlarge on one piece of yourself to create a whole new person.

One of the most important things in creating realistic characters is knowing more about them than you put on the page. Think of it as "back story." You may not write about what your characters' idea for a perfect day is, but you should know. You should know what kind of childhood they had, what their dreams are, what they admire, what hurts them, what's in their refrigerator and their wallet and their closet. When you write from that place of authority, your characters will feel real to both you and the reader; all that knowledge will support your story without being visible—kind of like good underwear.

All of this is not to say that you will necessarily know your characters fully before you start writing. They will very likely seem a bit vague at first, but as you live and work with them—putting them with other people, and in various situations, and perhaps occasionally dreaming of them at night—you will learn more and more about them. You will then come to that happy point where your characters begin leaving parts of themselves for you at unexpected moments—they'll ring the doorbell and run away, and there on the stoop will be some illuminating aspect of themselves, some why or wherefore that will help you see and understand them, thereby helping you to tell your story. What I mean is, you'll be at the grocery store, waiting in line, not thinking about your writing at all, and suddenly you'll know something else about your character: Some piece of knowledge about them will just fall into your head. Or, again while waiting in line, you'll see something that will inspire a thought about your character—someone you see wearing a red hat lets you know that your character's favorite color is red, that she in fact has a bedroom painted red and uses red satin sheets. You can even see something that can be used directly: The cashier sneezes in a spectacular way that fits your character perfectly.

The best way to learn how to write about people is to study them. Get in the habit of watching them, really paying attention to what it is about people that makes them uniquely themselves. If you're the kind of person who can sit in an airport and be more entertained by the people around you than by a magazine or newspaper, you're well on your way. One of the better writers I know also teaches writing. She's always short on time, and I once asked her if she were at least able to work on her own stuff when she give her students long, in-class assignments. "Oh no," she said. "I'm too busy looking at their foreheads and their shoes and the way they hold their pens." Well. There you have it.

When you're people-watching, do more than take in the details they present to you. Take one of those details and run with it. If you see a person in the airport who is very well dressed and carrying expensive luggage, what else might you deduce about her? Is her home luxurious? Imagine it: Where is it? How—and where—does she eat breakfast? Does she have children? Failed dreams? Weird allergies? Who are her parents?

When you see any given man walk past, give him a job, a wife, a dog, a hobby. Something about the man should dictate what you would write; in other words, if you were to then watch another man and assign him the same things, the list would be entirely different.

Look at photographs of people and imagine their voices; decide how they chew. Concentrate on one detail of anyone's physical presence, and imagine all that it can provide you. For example, you see a man with a really big nose.

What can be "done" with that nose? Is the guy's snore different? Has his nose always been big—did he suffer for its size when he was a kid? Is there someone who thinks it's beautiful? The more you work (or play, really) at freeing up your imagination and letting it run, the easier—and more enjoyable—it will be to conjure up vivid and believable characters.

PLOT

There are two kinds of writers, those who start with a plot and those who end up with one. I am one of the latter.

It just doesn't work for me to try to plot a novel. The few times I tried, it was as though the book rebelled—it went another way entirely, and then all those notes I'd taken to follow that ever-so-neat sequence of events I'd planned were in vain.

For me, part of the joy in writing fiction is the surprise of it, the discovery of things I hadn't known were in me or that I wanted to say, or, more likely, the way those things chose to be said.

When I write a novel, I start with a feeling. It's a strong feeling, but that's all it is. There's something I very much want to say and/or understand, and I need a novel to help me do it. In the case of *Durable Goods*, my first novel, I wanted to understand how it is that you can strongly love someone you're very much afraid of; and I wanted to bring compassion to a character many might find hard to forgive. In exploring those things, a plot emerged, of how a young girl transcends a childhood full of sorrow and pain and ends up full of hope.

But that plot only emerged because I started writing in the narrator's voice. I didn't know where she was going. But I let her lead anyway. (And for those of you who fret over beginnings, thinking they must be miniature masterpieces, consider that the first line in *Durable Goods* is the narrator saying, "Well, I have broken the toilet.")

I find almost nothing more enjoyable than to be working on a novel and wake up not having any idea what's going to happen that day. It keeps me interested. It keeps me excited. And I hope it keeps my readers interested, too. If I had to write what the plot told me was "up" next, I'd be bored—it would feel too much like homework.

That's not to say I don't keep notes when I'm writing a novel. I begin with a slim folder that ends up being crammed full of things written on napkins, on grocery lists, on backs of envelopes. Maybe I'll see a story in the newspaper that inspires me, that seems in some way to fit in with the story I'm writing, and I'll cut that out and throw it in the folder, too. Maybe I'll find a penny on the sidewalk on a day I'm taking a walk and thinking about the novel—that penny can get taped to the front of the folder. I might get a particular fortune in a cookie that I "need"; I might find a photograph in a magazine that looks exactly the way I imagine a character's bathtub looks. All these things get kept until they are used in the story—and sometimes they are kept after that.

After I start writing in earnest and I have a good thirty pages or so, the book graduates to a three-ring binder, but the binder must have a pocket, so it can hold things I continue to throw in.

The best thing that can happen to me when I'm writing fiction is to lose sight of the fact that I'm writing at all. It's as though I enter into a kind of trance. I know I'm writing, but I don't *think* about it. I just let my fingers type—it's as though the feeling comes out directly through them, bypassing the brain altogether. When that happens, I feel completely transported. There is nothing else like this feeling, very little else more important to me. That intimacy I feel between myself and my work is what makes me feel at home on the earth. I am basically a shy person, basically a loner and an outsider; and I have been all my life. But when I achieve the kind of connection I can get through writing, I feel I'm sitting in the lap of God.

On the best writing days, the pages fly by. Later, when I print out those pages and read them, I have no memory of having written the words. They're just there.

There is a great variety of books available that will tell you all about writing other ways, including adhering to a plot; and if you're the kind of writer who feels he or she needs that, I urge you to consult those sources. Everyone works differently, and I'm sure there are brilliant writers we both admire who would be horrified at the notion of writing without knowing where something is going—and how. But for me, the magic in writing fiction comes from taking that free fall into the unknown, and rather than making things happen, *letting* them.

GETTING STARTED

So much for all the ideas about theory and magic. How about a little practical advice? How can you really make the transition from nonfiction to fiction? What's a good first step?

You might want to start by writing about something that happened to you, enhanced by a few things that didn't: what you *wish* had happened at that time, for example. Or what you were afraid was going to happen. Or what it would have been like if it had turned out completely different.

For example, if you are married, consider your wedding day. What would it have been like if you hadn't gone through with it? Write the day as you remember it, from the time you woke up until just before the "I do"; then say "I don't." And write the rest of the scene. If you're not married, think of some similar turning point in your life, and write a scene taking a radically different road. Whatever you choose to write about, you're starting with a framework of reality, then fleshing it out with fictional detail. Think of writing "faction." As you gain more experience writing fiction, it will be easier to create things from the ground up.

When you are starting to write your first piece of fiction, try not to think about it too much beforehand, the way you probably do with nonfiction. Just go ahead and get started—with anything. Jump in—in the middle of a scene, if you want to—you can go back and put in a beginning later. (It may happen, though, that you want to keep a beginning that starts in the middle of a scene—that actually can be quite appealing.) You can start with a line of dialogue. A description of a place or a person. Anything!

Read the following first lines. What would you write next?

"I am alone here."

"He would not have been my first choice for a dog."

"My mother had a very peculiar habit."

"At twelve o'clock noon, everything started to happen."

If you feel intimidated at the thought of beginnings, grab the bull by the horns and write a *page* full of them—nothing but one sentence after the other that could be used for a beginning. Do this quickly, and don't worry about really using any particular sentence as a beginning (although of course you can).

Once you've gotten that first sentence down, unfasten your seat belt and get free. Let anything happen. Enjoy yourself. I know there are thousands of writers who complain about how difficult it is to write, how they hate it, how the only thing they like is having written, not the writing itself. But I'm not one of them, and you don't have to be, either.

Think of writing fiction as theatrical improvisation where you get to be all the characters. And the director. *And* the audience.

When improvisational actors come together for the first time onto a bare stage, everyone's cold. No one knows each other, or how they will work together, or what to expect. But then one character says something that gets the ball rolling, and then another character says something else, and the way that it's said helps determine what happens next. And at the end of the first run-through the director steps in and gives her two cents worth, helps shape the thing in another way.

To extend the analogy a bit: Don't expect your actors to perform at their best before they've become comfortable on the stage and with each other; and don't critique until a run-through is complete; that is to say, don't direct or be audience to your own work too soon.

When you write fiction, try hard to trust in your own unique creative process, and be open to being surprised. Be willing to relinquish a little control—if something else seems to want to take over, let it. See what it can offer you.

P. L. Travers said, "When I write, it's more a process of listening." Perhaps invoking the muse requires nothing more than temporarily stilling our own usual voices—both inside and out.

THE DAILY ROUTINE

Your routine for writing should be as personal and as varied as your routine for anything else. But there are a few general things that may be helpful to know.

For one thing, be aware that your routine may change as your life does, especially when you're a parent. When I first started writing, my hours for work were dictated by my children's schedules. When they were gone—to school, to camp, out to play—I could write. When they were there, I could not. (If I tried, both the writing and the kids suffered.) As it happened, that was fine. When my children were very young, I was writing essays that didn't require nearly the time and dreamy concentration that novels do. If I had a small child now, I'd probably have to use day care.

I think it's helpful to start every new writing day by reading yesterday's work, and editing that before you begin the new stuff. It needs to be done anyway, and it's a good warm-up.

When you're writing something, I think it's important to read many other things (so long as they are not similar to what you're doing), and to keep your mind always open for material that can enrich or inspire your own work, however indirectly. A book on elephants, for example, gave me exactly what I needed for an important passage in *Talk Before Sleep*, a book about a group of women friends who help one of their own through cancer. Watching a squirrel out my kitchen window gave me an idea for an important scene in *Range of Motion*. Some people say it is good practice to read only nonfiction when you're writing fiction, but I could *never* do that, so I won't tell you to.

I want to emphasize again the importance of not talking too much about what you're doing before it's written. It's like opening the oven too much when a cake is baking— the thing can fall. I remember telling a very good friend about a scene I planned to write for *Durable Goods*. When I finished describing it, she wrinkled her nose and said, "Well . . . to be honest, I don't think *that*'s a very good idea." It took a lot of courage for me to stand by that scene, to put it in anyway, and I'm very glad that I did. But don't set yourself up for that kind of thing—when a story is in the fragile forming state, still wet, so to speak, let your hands be the only ones to touch it.

Try very hard to love your work as you do it. This is important. Even as children thrive and flourish when parents show them love and acceptance, so does your own creativity. This is not to say you should not edit your work, not be willing to cut page after page, if necessary. But in your first draft, be as gentle and as accepting as you can be. Be very kind to yourself. It's risky, what you're doing. It's brave. It's good. Reward yourself with a pat on the head before you say you feel like putting a gun to it.

The purpose of a first draft is to get something down. That's all. Maybe it will turn out to be something that works so well you won't change a word—that happens. Maybe it will turn out so bad that virtually nothing gets kept. That's fine, too—it served its purpose in getting you going. As far as I'm concerned, every first draft gets an A+.

Realize that there can be a lot of going back and forth on how you feel about what you write. One day you write something and you think, *Wow! I got it! This is It; this is so right, this is FABULOUS!* Then the next day you read the same thing and think, *Oh my God, what was I thinking? This is garbage.* Probably it's not garbage. But maybe it's not so fabulous, either. See what you think on day three. And keep in mind the value of saving things you feel at first like throwing away. You don't have to save them forever—just don't destroy them right away.

A lot of people believe you must "murder your darlings." That is, if you write something that you think is really, really fine, it's probably far from it. Frankly, I haven't found that to be true. My darlings remain my darlings and I am happy never to have murdered one of them. However: I don't have all that many darlings.

One last thing. If you can't get to the place where you feel like you're having fun when you write fiction, at least make sure you feel interested. If you're not interested, you can be sure your reader will feel like tearing her hair out—if not yours.

Homework

Write two stories about how you came by an object that has a great deal of meaning to you. Make one nonfiction and one fiction. Give the stories to at least three people who don't know how you got that object, and ask them to tell you which story is true.

Make the Ocean Your Desk: Techniques for Getting Unstuck

> Saying you have "writer's block" is like saying, "Oh my God, I'm not hungry!"
>
> —ELIZABETH BERG

It would probably be too strong a statement for me to say I don't believe in "writer's block." But I *almost* don't believe in it. I think the term is a bit pretentious. I think everybody has days when his or her work is not flowing, no matter what that work is. But most people don't have the luxury of taking time off—they persevere and do the best they can; or, if it's really bad, they call in sick. I think that's what writers should do: If you have a day when you feel you can't write, don't write. Call in sick to yourself.

All of this is not to say that I'm unsympathetic to the feelings of anxiety and/or depression that can come when a writer simply can't write. I've had fallow periods myself. I know you can start thinking you've lost it; that it's never coming back; that you've said all you can ever say. But I've also learned that the best thing to do about being "blocked" is not to worry about it—to enjoy it, even. Think of it as a mandatory holiday. Go look at art; sit in an ice-cream parlor and eat a cone; visit a friend; see a movie; lie in bed with a great book and read. Most of all, remember this: If you have the calling to be a writer, it's not going to go away any more than the shape of your nose will. Your need and longing and ability to express yourself will come back. Like love, you can't force it. Like love, it will find you when it's ready. In addition to that, just because you're not putting pen to paper or fingers to computer keys doesn't mean you're not writing: If you are a writer and you're observing, you're working.

There are other times when you don't really feel "blocked," but you do feel stuck. You've been working away at something, making good progress, and then all of a sudden you hit a wall. You might know what you want to do down the road a ways, but you can't quite see what to do *next*. At times like this, a little stimulation can go a long way.

I once sat for a long time in front of my computer, trying to think of a way to start an article I had to write. I knew what I wanted to say in the middle and at the end, but the beginning was just not coming to me. I stared out the window and watched the trees move in the wind and thought. And thought. And nothing came. Finally, I gave up and turned my computer off. I decided to go for a walk and give up on writing for the day. Except: When I went for a walk, something in me woke up. I saw wonderful things: groups of pastel flowers at the edge of the road; gigantic cumulus clouds; a doe standing still as a statue, grass hanging out the sides of her mouth like whiskers. When I got home, I went back to the computer and wrote with ease. All I'd needed was a psychic change of position.

You can free yourself up simply by plunking yourself down in a different environment. Take your journal to the ocean. Sit on the sand close to the water, watch the constantly changing waveforms, and listen to the high cries of the seagulls. Write about everything you see and hear and feel, if only to make a list of sensations. Or go to a café, a hospital waiting room, a library, a church, and do the same. Walk through a shopping mall, looking not at the merchandise but the people: the overly made-up cosmetics saleswomen, the dispirited men who sell vacuum cleaners, the teenagers rifling through CDs, the young mothers window-shopping and pushing their babies in state-of-the-art strollers.

Bring a box of dog biscuits to the inmates at the humane society; lean up against a headstone in a graveyard and write about the feelings you have reading various epitaphs; wander about the halls of a courthouse looking at the faces of people who would rather be almost anywhere else. Attend a high school reunion that is not your own; if it can be done with some measure of respect, attend the funeral of someone you didn't know. (Of course, have the good taste not to whip out your journal during the service.) Go to your mom's house. Go to a movie. Sit at a tiny table in one of the ubiquitous coffeehouses and fill your journal pages with anything that comes to you—the more free-form, the better.

Or, try writing with an absence of stimuli: in darkness, in absolute quiet, perhaps with a single candle lit. Or write with different kinds of music in the background.

You can jump-start yourself by wandering around a library, sampling bits of books from many different sections—read about cowboys and Colette, look at huge books of photography and tiny books of verse.

One of the most surprising, entertaining, and informative things I ever did was to have a "dialogue" with an object in one of my dreams. This was an exercise suggested by the instructor in a class on dreams that I took many years ago. She suggested we pick an object that showed up in a dream, and, on paper, have a dialogue with it. "Don't worry about what to 'make' it say," she said. "Just begin by asking it a question. It will answer with whatever it wants to tell you."

She was right. I'd had a dream in which I was working in a deli, and huge salamis loomed over my head. I wanted to know the significance of them, and so I wrote out a dialogue with salami. I began with the completely uninspiring question, "Salami, what are you doing in my dream?" Lo and behold, like a miracle, the salami "spoke." Really! I wrote out a whole conversation between that salami and me, and learned that what it represented was my longing to spend more time doing domestic things. I know this sounds wacky, but just try it.

Classes in general, in fact, are a good way to get stimulated. I'm not talking about writing classes—we'll talk about those later. I mean some extension class in something that interests you, however vaguely. Beginning Italian. French cooking. Oil painting. How to buy a house. I once took a class called "Know Your Car." The class was filled with women. At the end of the first night, the instructor asked if there were any questions. One woman raised her hand and asked how she could clean her battery. "It's *filthy!*" she said, and the instructor sighed.

If you usually type, try writing in longhand. If you usually sit at a desk, write lying down. If you usually write in the morning, write at night.

Retreats can be both restorative and stimulating. Jane Hamilton, one of my all-time favorite novelists, says, "I go to a writer's colony once a year and work all day and half the night. When I'm not working, I take long walks. I can get months of work done in two weeks that way."

As for me, once or twice a year, I go to an oceanside resort town an hour away from where I live, and stay for three or four days. I hole up in a beautiful room with soft furniture, lamps with shades like doll dresses, and wonderful views of the water. Sometimes I bring a typewriter; other times, I write longhand. I read, write, take long walks, shop a little bit, and eat whatever I feel like eating. (Actually, part of my ritual is to stop at a "candy house" on the way and pick out a box full of wonderful milk chocolates. I get assisted by Satan disguised as an old lady wearing a hair net; she wanders up and down the rich-smelling aisles with me, encouraging me to get more and more. And more. Anyway, I get a box of great candy, which I keep on the doily-covered dresser and leave open for viewing and tasting pleasure. Turtles and chocolate-covered cherries are the best. But you have to get some French mints, too.)

There are group retreats available where you are housed with other writers in some swell location. I have found those kinds of retreats to be productive, too, although they can be expensive. Usually, those attending come together at night to share their work, if they would like; and at one retreat I attended, there was a journal-writing workshop every morning that was terrific—you could show up in your jammies. The meals were restaurant quality, and there was a very satisfying sense of camaraderie that happened at dinnertime, the only time when we all "had" to be together.

Whether you go off alone or with other writers, I highly recommend an occasional getaway. I have never yet found it to be unproductive. I have written short stories on retreats, I've finished novels, and I've enriched myself by reading others for hours—poets, novelists, essayists, nonfiction writers, too. If you do go on a retreat, try to keep yourself open to going in a direction you hadn't anticipated. You may go to a retreat to work on a novel and find that you end up writing a short story or an essay or the beginning of a memoir.

As reading a book or a poem can be inspiring, so can reading a single quotation. Whenever you read a line or a brief passage you really love, consider writing it out on something as mundane as an index card or as lovely as handmade paper. Keep this collection of literary jewels in a box somewhere and at times when you feel "dry," take the box out and literally surround yourself with these powerful words.

I suppose I could go on and on with ideas that might work to stimulate you back into productivity, but I'm sure you get the point, which is this: When you feel stuck, *Don't worry!* Trust in an ongoing process that has a timetable and a method of its own. You may not be able to control the way your own creativity works, but you can have faith that it will not leave you.

Now for a bit of practical advice. First of all, if you can avoid it, try not to work with deadlines. I know this is hard, but try to avoid it anyway. As much as possible, write what you love, and *then* worry about selling it. I believe it's critically important to try for a certain church and state–like separation. Keep writing and the creative process away from the business end of things.

Understand that there may be times when you really need to rotate crops. Maybe you write only fiction, and that's all you *want* to write. Still, it may happen that the well is suddenly dry and you need to try something else: essays, for example. Similarly, if you do only nonfiction, and you feel stale, try writing something more fanciful. You don't have to show it to anyone if you don't want to. But it is good to shake things up a bit, to leave a familiar place if only to see it anew when you come back home.

Let me leave you with a story that I was told a long time ago and have thought of many times since. Once, when a great physicist was working on an extremely complex problem, he was having difficulty coming up with an answer. So he did a very sensible thing. He went outside and played Frisbee. And that, of course, is when the answer came to him.

Homework

1. Take your journal outside your normal working place to anywhere you like. Fill at least three pages there. Then come home and eat a chocolate-covered cherry.

2. Next time you feel stuck, celebrate. You are being given an important opportunity.

3. Buy a Frisbee. (A Frisbee-fetching dog wearing a neckerchief is optional, but highly recommended.)

> No one else can teach a writer how to write or how
> to use imagination; only life and experience can
> teach that, but he or she can and should be taught
> technique.
>
> —RUMER GODDEN

If I had to say only one thing about classes in writing, it
would be this: You don't need them. That's not to say I don't
think they can be extremely valuable. I have taken classes
in fiction writing, screenplay writing, and "writing from
your own experience"; but I didn't take any classes until
after I was published, and for me, that made a big difference. It kept me from being so vulnerable. It kept me from
paying too much attention to what · someone else said
before I fully understood myself as a writer.

If there's one thing I worry about when people take writing classes, it's that their confidence will be destroyed; their
wonderful, original impulses quashed. In the hands of a
bad teacher or a bad class, this can happen. One uniquely
talented man I know went to a very prestigious MFA program and ended up feeling so humiliated by what people
said about his work that he now sells real estate. My fond-
est hope is that one of his clients will someday say, "What a
wonderful twenty-five-by-twenty chef's kitchen with warm

cherry cabinets and Sub-Zero refrigerator. Could you write me a novel about it?"

It's only fair to say that I've also heard stories about people being wonderfully well nurtured in writing classes: One shy and self-deprecating woman in a terrific teacher's class was gently but firmly encouraged to keep going when she wasn't at all sure she should. Her first story was accepted into the *Agni Review,* then short-listed for an edition of *Best American Short Stories.*

What I would like to do in this chapter is to take a look at writing classes from both sides of the desk, to first present some thoughts about being a student, and then to hear from two teachers of creative writing classes. If, after reading the information here, you think maybe you'd like to take a class, by all means do. Just remember that when the teacher or other class members critique your work, it is an opinion you're hearing. Not a divination. Not a mandate. It may be right; it may be wrong; and it may be a little of both. You should try to listen objectively. You should try to learn things that will make you a better writer; you should be willing to try new things. But also try to have the inner strength to stand by something you believe in, no matter what anyone says.

WHAT KIND OF PEOPLE TAKE WRITING CLASSES?

It runs the gamut. You'll see everyone from nose-ringed teens to pastel-cardiganed grandmothers; from people who have published a fair amount to those who have never let anyone else see their work until now. Some people are painfully shy and quiet; others seem to believe that the reason there are others in the class is to provide an audience—not only for every word they write, but also for every opinion they have. Some people are wonderful writers, and some are really, really, really *not* wonderful. (Often, unfortunately, it's the ones who are not wonderful who think they are, and vice versa.) Some people are enthusiastic and conscientious and come to every class fully prepared. Others attend sporadically or drop out altogether.

WHAT KIND OF CLASS IS BEST TO TAKE?

This, of course, depends on what your interests are. There are classes on everything from magazine writing to those on how to submit your finished novel; classes on writing fiction, screenplays, memoir, and newspaper pieces; classes on keeping journals, on getting unstuck, and on how the numbers in the publishing industry work.

If you've never taken a class before, you might look for something general, such as "Writing for Publication" or "Writing Fiction." If you're working on something specific, chances are you'll be able to find a class that deals with that subject.

You can take day classes or evening classes; you can take them at colleges and universities, at adult education centers, in bookstores, and in people's homes. You can find information about classes posted on bulletin boards in bookstores and libraries, at the back of writing magazines, and in community course catalogues. Some classes meet only once; some meet for several weeks, or months, or longer.

Deciding on what class to take will have to do not only with your areas of interest, but also with how much time and money you have at your disposal.

WHAT SHOULD YOU EXPECT FROM A WRITING CLASS?

You should expect support. You should expect to learn some things you didn't know about the art of writing and the business of publication. You should expect insightful input on what you write. You should feel taken seriously, inspired to write more and better, and you should also be able to have some fun.

You should *not* expect that your instructor will be willing to:

1. Spend more time on your work than she does on that of others.

2. Use the contacts she may have to help get you published.

3. Stay after class to discuss concerns with you.

(It may be that your instructor *will* do all of the above, but you shouldn't *expect* it.)

Try to go into a class open-minded and optimistic, willing to listen and willing to learn. When it comes to commenting on other people's work, be honest but kind— which is probably exactly how you would like your own work to be commented upon. There's a very good chance that you'll get a lot out of a class and enjoy it very much; but if you start feeling less confident rather than more, if you begin to feel inhibited and ashamed or dumb, *quit!* That's an order from me to you.

WHO TEACHES WRITING CLASSES?

I'm sure you've heard the expression, "Those who can, do; those who can't, teach." Although there are some terrible writers who teach, my experience is that the teachers tend to be very good writers. Not all of them are very good teachers, however.

It takes real talent to teach anything, and it takes a particular kind of talent to teach writing. When people show others their writing, they are uniquely vulnerable, even those who have been published a great deal. A good writing teacher needs to inspire but not dictate, praise without making someone overconfident, and critique without humiliating or discouraging. Perhaps most important, teachers have to let their students write in their own way.

Many, if not most, writing instructors teach because they need the money. But I believe a lot of the best would teach whether they needed the money or not. Those teachers love teaching, love giving to other writers, and the ones I've met say they get a lot back.

I have two women friends who juggle their own writing with teaching various classes. I asked them to contribute to this book, and in an act of great generosity, they did. I had intended to summarize what they said—to offer you a literary casserole of their combined thoughts. But after I read the pages each of them gave me, I realized that my voice

summarizing them would deny you some of the most elo-
quent, passionate, inspired, and downright sensible writing
about teaching I've ever had the pleasure to read. These
women's words, more than anything else in this chapter,
will show you how taking a writing class with the right kind
of teacher can give you wings.

Jessica Treadway, author of an extremely fine and award-
winning collection of short stories called *Absent Without
Leave,* has also had short stories and book reviews published in *The Atlantic Monthly, Ploughshares, Glamour,* the
Boston Globe, and many other publications. She teaches
classes in fiction writing at Tufts University, Emerson College, and Harvard University's extension school. In response to a question about writing exercises, she said the
following:

> In terms of assignments, I usually start off with one that
> will allow students to practice writing, but also help
> them to get to know each other a little. Usually, they're
> strangers, for the most part, when they come to the
> classroom. And since most normal people are a bit ner-
> vous if not downright terrified at the prospect of being
> in a "creative writing" class, I want them to feel com-
> fortable with each other, and also get over, almost imme-
> diately, the formidable hurdle of reading their work
> aloud for the first time. The one that seems to work best
> as an icebreaker is the "My Name" exercise, based on a
> one-page excerpt from Sandra Cisneros's *The House on*

Mango Street. Basically, the narrator of the book introduces herself in this passage and tells how her name is tied to her family history and the way she thinks of herself. I ask students to write their own "My Name" exercise for the second class. It's not paralyzing, because just about everyone has a story or a feeling about his or her name, and it serves the purpose of reinforcing our learning each other's names. Some students do just their first names; some do middle, first, and last; some, in the spirit of the class, even write from the standpoint of a fictional character.

Other exercises: Observe a stranger—on the bus or in a café or in the waiting room at the doctor's office—and write a childhood memory from his or her point of view. This allows the student practice in "inhabiting" another person without having to invent that person first.

When asked about signs of real writing talent:

I always take special notice when a student hands in pages filled with emotion, original language, and ideas that may not be perfectly expressed but contain a certain quality—I call it "wildness"—that marks it distinctly and unmistakably as the author's own. Grammar, punctuation, and precision can be learned and honed. Wildness—the willingness to take risks and expose oneself—perhaps cannot (or it is at least, I believe, harder to acquire). I'll take a wild, exuberant fragment over a competent, dull, complete, sentence any day.

About what she encourages students to read:

I'm tempted to say that students should read *everything*, but that isn't the most practical advice—I mean, shouldn't we all? I do believe, however, that there's a certain vocabulary of works that serve us in discussing the contemporary short story and in writing it. I always include reading discussions in my syllabus, because I think the best way of illustrating different ways to "do" things in writing is to study examples in the context of published work by writers who know what they're doing. Some of the authors and stories I think are cornerstones of such a "vocabulary" are Joyce Carol Oates's *Where Are You Going, Where Have You Been?* (this is especially interesting to read alongside Flannery O'Connor's *A Good Man Is Hard to Find*); Tim O'Brien's "On the Rainy River" and "The Lives of the Dead"; Sherwood Anderson's *Winesburg, Ohio*; Andre Dubus's "A Father's Story"; Robert Coovers's "The Babysitter"; James Baldwin's "Sonny's Blues"; Amy Bloom's "Silver Water"; John Barth's *Lost in the Funhouse*; Raymond Carver's "The Bath" (with its expanded version, "A Small, Good Thing"), "Cathedral," and "Errand"; Kate Chopin's "The Story of an Hour"; John Cheever's "The Swimmer," "The Country Husband," and "The Enormous Radio"; Lorrie Moore's "How to Become a Writer"; Tillie Olsen's "I Stand Here Ironing"; Katherine Anne Porter's "The Grave"; John Updike's "A&P" and "Separating"; Tobias Wolff's "Hunters in the Snow" and "Bullet in the Brain"; Alice Munro's "Carried

Away"; Delmore Schwartz's *In Dreams Begin Responsibilities*; Tolstoy's "The Death of Ivan Iliych"; Mary Gaitskill's "A Romantic Weekend"; Denis Johnson's "Jesus' Son"; Robert Stone's "Helping". . . it goes on and on, of course. These authors and these stories have been an important part of my writing education.

Some miscellaneous advice:

One thing I always like to stress, from early on in any class, is the distinction (for the purposes of a fiction writing class, anyway) between facts and truth. As William Faulkner observed, they really don't have much to do with each other. Say a student turns in a manuscript containing some episode that another student finds "contrived." Invariably, the author's response is a triumphant, "But it really happened!" This may be a valid defense in the courtroom, but not in a fiction class. Just because an event occurred in real life doesn't automatically confer upon it the "ring of truth" that is so important in fiction. Conversely, if you write the scene well enough, you can convince your reader that pigs fly to the moon. (That's one of the best things about being a fiction writer—not only do you get to invent people, you can create the universes they live in, including its natural laws. Even gravity need not apply.)

Readers want to be seduced. The willingness to suspend disbelief is, I believe, a natural one for most people—we want to be drawn into other lives and stories, cultures, minds, worlds. It reinforces our view of ourselves as members of humanity; it reminds us of what we have in common with each other.

Writing that last paragraph makes me think of what happened when I saw *Titanic* with my friend Kathleen. On the screen, the ship approaches the iceberg; the lookouts can see the vast shape rising up out of the water. When they sound the alarm, the shipmates use all their might to steer the vessel out of harm's way. As we watched the iceberg come closer and closer, on the screen, Kathleen leaned over to me and said, "Are you hoping they don't hit it?" I thought for a second and realized that I was. "So am I," she told me. Remembering this makes me laugh every time. It doesn't take much to draw most of us into the suspense of a story, even when we know what will happen next. Engaging the reader at that level of emotional investment—making the drama so real that what we may "know" doesn't matter—is, I think, the writer's job.

On judging others' writing:

First of all, "creative" writing is so subjective, so much a matter of taste, that what doesn't appeal to me may very well capture the fancy of every other member of the class. Who's to say which is the "correct" response? The reading experience of another student is no less valid than that of a teacher. Of course, sometimes there are glaring gaps, insufficiencies, tacked-on endings, wholly unbelievable dialogue, or other examples of what one of my writing friends calls "howlers"—the things that make you, reading, cringe. (We all commit them, by the way—students, teachers, and Nobel Prize winners alike.) Nonetheless, there are ways to state your opinion without resorting to insults, cruelty, or sarcasm.

When I was in graduate school, we in the fiction class all waited, with bated breath, for the teacher to render his opinion of our stories. If they found favor with him, we beamed and crowed (pretending to be subtle about it, of course). If he blasted our work, we bit our lips, defended our metaphors, cried, or got drunk in the pub after class (the latter was my preferred method). The point was, we let him decide what was good and what wasn't. The last thing I want to do, as a teacher, is invite my students to endow me with such power. Who was he, and who am I, to say? Besides, even if we think students have a long way to go before publishing anything, who's to say that it's an impossibly long way? I always think of a particular student I had in my first semester of teaching graduate school. Her work was earnest, but if pressed, I'd have said she was among the less accomplished fiction writers in the class. During the next three years, while earning her degree, she practiced her craft and wrote hard, and by the time we met to discuss her thesis, she'd already published a story in *Redbook*. Talent isn't everything. And I think a good fiction writing class teaches you not so much how to write but how to work at writing.

The best thing about teaching fiction is that I get to sit around with good people, read stories, and talk about them—for a living. Sometimes—often—I can't believe how lucky I am. I can't imagine anything better than working with other people whose passion, like mine, is to touch hearts by means of putting words to paper. It feels honest and meaningful, which is a lucky thing to be able to say, in this day and age, about how one spends one's day.

If this writing is not proof that those who teach *can* write, I don't know what is. I wish you would take a break now. I wish you would go and lie down and close your eyes and think about the honesty, wisdom, good-heartedness, and absolute beauty of what you just read. Then come back for part two.

Alexandra Johnson is the award-winning author of *The Hidden Writer: Diaries and the Creative Life,* a book beautifully styled and written, as well as utterly inspiring. It belongs on every writer's bedside table. As a freelance writer, Alexandra has been published everywhere from *The New Yorker* to the *New York Times Book Review.* She teaches memoir and creative nonfiction at Harvard University's extension school. Here's how she responded to my questions about teaching:

I'm going to answer most of your questions, but first I have to add a kind of manifesto about teaching, trust, and the power dynamic that's at work in most classes.

The most important thing any student can do when

looking for a writing workshop is to make sure the person who's teaching it is a real writer. The prospective student should read the instructor's work beforehand—not for brownie points, but to get a sense if this is someone for whom he or she feels trust and respect.

The best teachers of writing I know are, in fact, some of the best writers I know. Their teaching is good because they've spent years struggling with the very problems students are there to work through: finding story ideas, learning to shape narrative, anchoring it with concrete and sensory details. They are able to take students through all the stages of writing and rewriting because that's what they do daily. They're also good teachers because they're generous. Often (but not always) the more famous the writer, the more generous the teacher. For example, Nobel Prize–winner Seamus Heaney brings all his horrible early drafts to class to show students how long it takes to get to the final published poem. And he's willing to listen to students' most basic concerns.

Beware the writing teacher who doesn't write. This could be an editor, an agent, etc. There are plenty of such teachers who are good, but they often teach from a highly detached, highly intellectual, and critical place.

Beware, too, teachers who may be well published but who don't encourage. Sadly, there are a lot of these around. Writing workshops can be their chance to feel more powerful in the face of students whose early work is easy to criticize. I know teachers who, consciously or subconsciously, are actually jealous of promising work and can spend an entire semester nitpicking a student's work to death.

Examples: A teacher in a top MFA program wanted his students to meet in a area where there was coffee nearby. The real purpose was to take a woman's story, put it in the nearby microwave, and zap it. "This story is half-baked," he said, holding up her charred draft to a giggling but nervous class. The woman left the program.

Recently, a former memoir student of mine told me about her new fiction class. The teacher spends the entire time carving up everyone's stories. Okay, maybe they need work. But then he takes a number of stories published in *Best American Stories* and hacks those to death. What is anyone learning in that class? Misanthropy? How to be a critic? Many promising writers could easily get discouraged, thinking it's their problem.

Students should, if possible, read past course evaluations. They should trust their instincts about a teacher. And about a class.

Members of the good classes often feel they want to form a future writing group with a number of the other members. Part of what makes classes good is learning what criticism to accept as valid, and what is just someone's personality tic; for example, the person who reorders a draft whether or not it needs it. I always ask, "Does it make it better or just different?" Often, it's just different. And sometimes wrong.

The best students will come wanting to make their work better. They're willing to go through a zillion drafts if it will make the work good. They care deeply about their stories.

Students any teacher gets nervous about? Ones who have an eye for 1) being famous immediately, and 2) getting published yesterday.

Beware the students who don't read. Who won't read. How will they ever learn to write? Beware students as consumers who sit listening to discussions about technique, etc., yet are too lazy to try them out each week. Those students wait for the teacher to edit the work rather than making it better on their own. Nightmare students try to dominate the discussions; routinely don't follow assignments; talk about themselves a lot—including when they are supposedly workshopping someone else's work.

I find the best students—the ones whose drafts you'd show your own editor—are always hardest on their work. They're often underconfident. They're perfectionists with high internal critics. Example: I had a student who'd never gone to college but already was beginning to write essays for a local paper. Her work was wonderful but she was a slow, slow writer. With recommendations from another creative writing teacher and myself, she skipped college and went right into a top MFA program. You feel then, as a writer and as a teacher, that you really helped someone help herself.

I try to teach as I wish someone had taught me (I never took a writing course). I talk a lot about the psychological voices—the internal critic, the perfectionist, the procrastinator. I try to have students begin with short assignments—no more than two pages—and build up to longer. I give them models each week, from published writers and former students, as guides to crafting that week's assignment.

Writing classes/workshops are great in that they give a student weekly deadlines—get the work going. Good classes give you a lot of suggestions about what's already working in the draft and what, specifically, needs to be revised. And how to do it. What's exciting is seeing fourteen people brainstorming about someone's work, often making connections even the writer hadn't gotten in an earlier draft.

At the beginning of every fiction workshop I tell the following story: Several years ago I had a student who really wanted to write. She'd done poetry, but not a lot else. She needed to learn how to shape a story, to be more concrete. That class had some of the best writers in it I'd ever had. This woman did okay in the class, but she wasn't in the top percentile. After my class, she began to take every writing class she could. She took a class again with me in her junior year. I couldn't believe it was the same writer. By the time she'd graduated, she'd won every fiction award at Harvard. Had you asked me in the first class who was going to be the writer, I'd have said the girl who ended up a doctor or the guy who is now working as a screenwriter. I never would have said that other student. Yet she was the one who actually pulled it off.

I know those of you who may want to take a class won't necessarily have anyone like either of these two remarkable writers for teachers. But in reading what they have to say, you have learned a lot about what to look for. And what to avoid.

Homework

Find out about at least five kinds of writing classes being offered in your area. Learn course content and find out what the teacher's background is.

> . . . That writers are special people. In fact we're most of us quite ordinary, only—well-suited or not—equipped with the habit of art, a susceptibility to language, a practice of noticing, a faith in writing itself learned from reading.
>
> —RICHARD FORD, UPON BEING ASKED WHAT HE BELIEVED TO BE THE GREATEST MYTH ABOUT BEING A WRITER

Much—if not most—of this book has been devoted to myth busting, in one way or another. But here is a concentrated list of things I hear over and over, and don't believe—and why I don't believe them.

1. WRITING IS HARD

For some, it is. For many, it is. But for others, it isn't. Don't let someone else's ideas about writing shape your own experience prematurely; don't let other's weary admonitions about the difficulty they've had in doing something in particular discourage you from trying it yourself.

From the first, you may indeed agree with many that writing is terribly hard—and often greatly frustrating—work. You may even eventually emulate those writers who advise people who want to write to consider doing almost anything else.

But, you may, also from the first, find writing to be a relief, even an exercise in sustained joy. Understand that to love writing rather than suffer from it is a valid option, and nothing to be ashamed of. Because, believe me, if you do love writing, if you find it easy and joyful, and you admit to that, there are plenty of people who can make you feel ashamed, whether they intend to or not.

I've heard too many times from people who thought things they wrote couldn't possibly be any good because those things came too easily, because the writers did not sit morosely at their desk, squeezing out words like drops of blood. Similarly, I'm sick to death of the raised-eyebrow snobbery shown by some writers—and many critics—who believe that writing anything *must* take a long time, and the but-of-course academically spawned writer *should* suffer in one way or another in creating it. Written with ease does not mean written badly.

I am fully aware that many people find writing to be hard work. I am also aware that a lot of writers deny the inherent joy in working hard at something they love, and feel they must instead affect a certain artsy anguish in order to earn satisfaction, whether that is from themselves, their peers, or their audience.

The truth is, we all occasionally encounter difficulties in what we write, for one reason or another. We all have days when the work doesn't flow; or when we reach a level of psychic exhaustion early on; or when we just keep missing the thing we need to hit. But when I hear people moan and groan about how much they hate writing, how awful it is, I always think, *Well, for God's sake, why do it, then? Why not take your hand out of the fire? Why not go find something you like doing?*

2. IT'S HARD TO GET PUBLISHED

Again, for some, it is; for others, it isn't.

When you're talking about being published, remember that there is a vast difference between submitting something to a major book publisher or mainstream magazine and offering a piece of fiction to a small magazine, or an essay to a newspaper. Don't say it's impossible to get published until you've tried a variety of venues. (Remember: There are around 5,000 literary magazines alone in this country!)

Remember, too, that although the number of writers being published versus the number of writers submitting is a grim statistic, it has nothing to do with you as an individual. Why? First of all, when you consider only yourself, the statistic becomes either zero or 100 percent. (What I mean is this: Say the odds of your being published by *McCall's* magazine are one in two hundred. In the end, it only means a piece is taken—100 percent— or it isn't—zero.)

Second, remember that *any*one can submit *any*where, unless a place has a policy that it does not look at un-agented material. But many, if not most, magazines and some publishing houses still look at over-the-transom (unsolicited) submissions. I've talked to a number of editors and publishers about this, asking if it's not actually exciting to go through the slush pile, knowing that in those huge piles, there's always the possibility of finding a real gem. Uniformly, editors have sighed and said no, it's not exciting; that although there have been cases where terrific manuscripts have been found, most of what's in the slush pile is absolutely terrible. The happy news about this is that if you can write at all well, your odds are automatically greatly improved.

3. YOU HAVE TO KNOW SOMEONE TO GET PUBLISHED

It's true that it might help to know someone in the business, or to have someone refer you to an editor or agent. But in the end, it's your own talent that's going to get you somewhere. And I firmly believe that if you do have talent, and you get your work out there, you *will* get published.

4. YOU HAVE TO HAVE CREDITS TO GET PUBLISHED

Elizabeth Crow, who was an editor at *Parents* magazine and is now at *Mademoiselle,* published me with no credits at all. I think it is true of most magazine editors that they are willing to take a chance on someone who's not yet been published. Sally Koslow, editor in chief at *McCall's,* says, for example, "I'm thrilled to publish a talented unknown." Keith Bellows, editor in chief of *National Geographic Traveler,* says, "I love it! My biggest delight is to take chances on people, to stay open to unknowns."

Of course, before you submit anything to a magazine, you must afford its editor the courtesy of being familiar with her or his publication. Sally Koslow says, "If you want to write for magazines, begin by reading magazines (and books and newspapers, too). If you don't love magazines, pick another form of writing. Before you pitch to a particular magazine, read as many issues of it as you can find, and learn to identify its heart and soul." Regarding proposals, she said, "I look for a sharp, targeted pitch that shows an awareness of *McCall's* and the *McCall's* reader. Show that you know the magazine. Package the query with a grabby working title and a succinct summary of what the story offers. What's new about it? Why is the story compelling? And is the story an exclusive to *McCall's*? My dream writer has a fluid style, works quickly, respects deadlines, gets her facts straight, writes to the word length assigned, has her finger on the pulse of what's newsy for our readers—and has a great sense of humor in her dealings with me, if not on paper."

Keith Bellows says, "Show me you can tell a story; don't pitch the subject so much as the story. I look for a sense of uniqueness, and pieces that come out of real-life experiences. I like a writer to show a sense of humor about the world."

5. YOU HAVE TO HAVE AN AGENT

When and if you have a book-length manuscript (or if you've been published quite a bit and you have a partial manuscript) you should consider acquiring an agent. If what you're marketing are articles and short stories, however, you don't need one.

You will often hear that an agent wants you to have a list of publishing credits before she will consider you. But many agents are happy to look at a proposal and a chapter or two, even if you haven't been published yet. As a rule, do not send the entire manuscript unless you are asked to.

I was given the name of my agent by Elizabeth Crow, who had by then published a great number of my magazine pieces. If you have no clue where to find an agent, look on the acknowledgment pages of published books you admire. Authors often thank their agents on these pages. Other places to consult are *Writer's Market, Literary Market Place,* Jeff Herman's *Writer's Guide to Book Editors, Publishers and Literary Agents,* or the back pages of literary or writing magazines. You should not have to pay a fee to have your work considered.

As eager as you may be to have an agent, remember that the most important thing for you to do is write. Put the work of creating ahead of the work of finding representation. If you finish a novel and you can't find an agent, remember that you can always submit it yourself—or publish it yourself, for that matter. More than one unagented and/or self-published book has been picked up by a big house and gone on to the *New York Times* bestseller list. *The Christmas Box* is one such success story.

6. FIRST DRAFTS ARE ALWAYS TERRIBLE

It is true that, most of the time, your work will improve with rewriting. And it is also true that a lot of first drafts really *are* terrible. But I believe that, in general, first drafts have gotten a bad rap; I think there's often a great deal more of good, usable stuff in them than people admit or allow themselves. Moreover, there's likely to be a kind of freshness and honesty in them, and perhaps the likeable straightforwardness and lack of pretense you find in children's writing as well. Don't be too quick to trash a first draft, to assume that there's very little in it that you can actually use. And *never* throw it away until you're completely satisfied that the rewritten version has extrapolated all it can from its birth mother, and truly is better than the original.

7. WHEN YOU'RE WRITING, YOU HAVE TO KNOW WHERE YOU'RE GOING

Surely, by now, enough writers have said that when they're writing, they *don't* know where they're going. Surely it's time for this myth to die a natural death. But the belief has persisted among many that no matter what you're doing, you have to have a clear idea of where you're headed.

As far as I'm concerned, the less you know about where you're headed, the better, at least when you're writing fiction. Trying to know too much about where you're going takes all the fun out of getting there. Lao-tzu (570–490 B.C.) said, "A good traveler has no fixed plans and is not intent on arriving." That's some of the best advice on writing—and life—I've ever read. It's all in the journey. Take your time, listen more to your heart than your head, and let your writing shape itself into what it wants to be.

8. YOU HAVE TO BE DISCIPLINED TO BE A WRITER

What you have to be is in love. With writing. Not with ideas about what to write; not with daydreams about what you're going to do when you're successful. You have to be in love with writing itself, with the solitary and satisfying act of sitting down and watching something you hold in your head and your heart quietly transform itself into words on a page.

9. THE PUBLISHING WORLD IS FULL OF JERKS

In my experience, the publishing world is full of generous and excited people who love reading and writing and writers, and who love what they do. I have had more experience with nasty writers than with nasty editors, agents, or publishers.

Don't approach people in publishing with a negative attitude. Understand that they're people who have good days and bad days, prejudices and weaknesses just like you. It is in their best interest to find and keep good writers; that's their job. They do not derive pleasure from rejecting people; it takes time away from what they want to do, which is find and publish good writers. Understand that their desks are piled with things to be taken care of right now, all the time. Sally Koslow of *McCall's* says, "My normal work day starts at nine and ends at six. I can count on nonstop meetings, brainstorming sessions, phone calls and e-mails, which are interrupted by a business lunch. Not a minute to breathe. Many evenings and every weekend I truck home manuscripts and proposals—I rarely have enough uninterrupted time at the office to read. Several times a month or on the weekend there is an work-related evening activity. My work usually follows me on vacation, too. I don't know one editor in chief whose hours are anywhere close to nine to five." Book editors and agents are no different; they, too, work very hard. So give them a break. Don't expect an immediate response from them, especially if they've never heard of you. If you send something to them and don't hear back in six weeks or so, send a follow-up letter rather than calling.

10. IF ONLY I COULD . . . , I'D HAVE IT MADE

It is my belief that the more success you enjoy, the more challenge and insecurity you can feel. That's not to say I don't think you shouldn't want to be successful, or that I don't feel gratified and nourished by my own success. It's only to say that I don't believe there ever comes a time when an artist (or probably anyone else who endeavors to do a job with passion) is completely satisfied. I remember thinking that if only I could get published *once*, I'd have everything I wanted. I'd be fully satisfied.

Well. It *was* wonderful getting published that first time. Turned out that it wasn't exactly all I wanted, though.

11. WORK ON IT UNTIL IT'S RIGHT

This is good advice that I have too often seen taken to extremes. Some writers become so caught up in the idea of making a piece perfect that they are never willing to let it leave their hands. Or they revise it so much it loses its original spark, its life.

The truth is, it's very rare that you feel a finished piece is *exactly* right. But there's a point after which it does not pay to tinker with it anymore. Rather than working on a piece until it's "right," work on it until you feel it's the best you can do. For me, there's a kind of internal relaxation that occurs when that happens, a natural inclination to lift the hands from the page. Pay attention to such indicators in yourself. They are there. Learn to trust them.

12. WHAT'S DEPRESSING DOESN'T SELL

My most commercially successful novel, *Talk Before Sleep*, is about a woman who dies from breast cancer, and you know from the beginning that she's going to die. The magazine pieces I wrote that generated the most admiring reader mail were about "depressing" topics.

There's nothing wrong with feeling sad about things, as a writer or as a reader. There are things in the world we *should* feel sad about. But when you write about such things, I believe it's important to show what might be called spiritual integrity. Don't write things that make people ache inside without some higher purpose: Give them something back, let their emotional risk-taking have been worthwhile. Perhaps your intent is to illuminate something; perhaps you want to spur people into action for a good cause. But you should never fill people with despair for no reason, any more than you should write gratuitous violence. In my opinion, that kind of writing is malevolent manipulation.

13. A GOOD WAY TO LEARN TO WRITE IS TO COPY A FEW PAGES OF AN AUTHOR YOU ADMIRE, WORD FOR WORD

Every time I hear this advice, I want to scream. What is this particular exercise meant to achieve? Envy? Despair? Why waste your time copying someone when you could be mining your own rich veins? If you copy a page created by an author you greatly admire, aren't you then intimidated about going back to your own words? Especially since you'll probably go from a very much finished piece of an esteemed writer right into a first draft of your own words. *Eeeeyikes!*

I know this technique is offered as a way of making a writer feel empowered, or as a method for "getting going," but I think if you must resort to it, you should use your *own* words. Copy something of your own that you like. Or copy the words of an author you hate, and then be filled with confidence that you can do *much* better than that!

Someone once asked me, "But wouldn't you be flattered if someone were copying your words out on a page?" I said I would be happy if someone admired my work, but I would not like to have it copied. It's too much like the way the rocks of Sedona get stolen and brought back to New Jersey. Not that there's anything wrong with New Jersey. It's just that the rocks belong to Sedona. And New Jersey has its own charms. (I mean this. I hate those New Jersey jokes. I *like* New Jersey.)

Homework

All right. This has been a very crabby chapter. In a most magnanimous gesture, I am giving you an assignment that *may* prove me wrong. Your homework is to copy a page of writing you admire and then, in the spirit of this book, make your own decision about whether it works to inspire you.

10 *Writing Groups*

It is not often that someone comes along
who is a true friend and a good writer.
—E. B. WHITE, FROM *CHARLOTTE'S WEB*

The act of writing is a solitary thing. But it doesn't have to be completely solitary. Writing groups offer you a chance to run works-in-progress past other writers, for honest evaluation and for support. The best groups have members who share interests, goals, levels of tolerance—even temperaments.

The first time I joined a writing group, I was terrified. When my story was read aloud, I wasn't sure I could stay in the room until its completion. And when I listened to what the other people said about it, I only half heard them—I was too busy inwardly squirming, outwardly blushing.

This got better in that I was soon able to hear and take in everything everyone said. (I don't mean that I *took* every suggestion; I only mean that I could hear every suggestion.) But the fear never leaves you. Only last night I was at a meeting of my writing group, sitting around with women whom I've been meeting with for years. In this group, we read our own work aloud, and at one point we talked about how this is *still* hard to do. I said I always feel like inserting

"I'm sorry; I'm sorry," between each sentence, and they nodded empathetically.

No matter what your level of experience, it is always an act of real trust to put new work out before other writers, live and in person. You feel rather like you've unwrapped your newborn and lain him down in the middle of a circle of people who just happen to have rocks in their hands. Many fine writers I know have told me they wouldn't dream of being in a writing group. These writers keep their cards close to their chest—their editors are the only ones who see their books before the public does.

I can see the value in letting no one interfere with your work in any way; I can understand the need for it. But my overall experience with writing groups is so positive, I would encourage anyone who is at all interested or curious to at least try one.

WHO'S IN A WRITING GROUP?

Everyone from people who have never been published to those who have many books and/or other publishing credits on their résumé. (The number of writing credits you have has nothing to do with how valuable your input to a group is, by the way. Some of the best advice I've gotten has come from people who have published nothing. Similarly, some of the worst has come from people who have had plenty of publishing success.) Ages can vary widely—I've been in groups where people range from their twenties to their sixties.

There are groups that are all one sex; and there are those that are mixed. I have been in both and find that although a man's point of view is of great value, I prefer, and tend to profit more from, all-women groups.

Some groups are made up only of published writers. I think to exclude people because they have not yet been published is a big mistake. What I look for in a writing group member is good writing, honesty, intelligence, sensitivity, a good sense of humor, and fine cooking skills. Not necessarily in that order. Perhaps most important, a good group member is that most old-fashioned and wonderful of things: kind. That means she has an ability and willingness to be careful not only with another writer's words, but with that person's heart.

HOW DO WRITING GROUPS WORK?

This depends, of course, on who the people in the group are, and what they decide about how they want to operate. Some groups meet monthly, some weekly. They come together in people's houses (picking one group member's house or alternating), libraries, bookstores, cafés, or other public places. They may have one person read per meeting, or two; or all the members (if all read, there must of course be a limit on the number of pages presented).

Some groups are made up of only three or four people; some are as large as twelve. Some groups combine a potluck dinner with working; some have snacks available; some don't have any food at all, seeing it as an unnecessary distraction. (I could *never* be in that kind of group.)

Sometimes members read their own work; sometimes they read each other's; sometimes a paid leader (who does not read her own work) reads everyone else's, and guides the discussions. If you do have a paid leader, she should be knowledgeable not only about literature, but about group dynamics as well.

Group meetings last anywhere from an hour to three or four. Sometimes the group is very social, and there's a fairly long time spent chatting before people get down to work. Other times, people want to get serious right away.

The best way to solicit comments from a group is to provide everyone with a copy of what is being read. Then people can write comments directly on the page, wherever and whenever they please.

When offering suggestions, it's important that you be honest, but it's equally important that you remember the vulnerability of the writer whose work you are reading. Try to start by saying something you like before you get into what does not work for you. (This is something I confess I am not good at, because I am a tactless Sagittarian who has to *rush* right in with my opinion about the way I think things should go. I *do* get around to saying what I like later, but I am trying to remember to do it the other way around.)

In critiquing, what is looked at is everything—from how a piece affects someone reading it to the mechanics of how it is written. In our group, as we listen to the pages being read, we put a check mark by anything we like. (It feels great when you go home and consolidate all the remarks on one copy, and see that a passage you weren't sure about is so covered with check marks it looks like a little field of grass.) If we feel something *doesn't* work for some reason or another, we'll bracket it. Other, more general (or more complicated), things are handled in the discussion after the piece is read. The person being critiqued knows that her job is to listen to these comments, then "take what you need and leave the rest."

My group, made up of five A+ women, meets weekly at a member's house. We start at seven in the evening; everyone who has material reads; and we are usually finished by nine or nine-thirty. We eat. We chat. We drink wine and/or tea. We really like each other—we have, in fact, become very good friends. Going to my writing group is one of the things I look forward to most every week. I rely on it for many things I couldn't do without. I am grateful for the ongoing sustenance I get there; and I hope to stay in this group or one like it until I'm 102. Although then the snacks will all have to be puréed.

WHAT ARE THE BENEFITS OF BEING IN A GROUP?

There's nothing like knowing a group meeting is coming up to get you writing. It's a deadline, in a way, but a nonthreatening one.

Almost without exception, members of a group will catch things in your manuscript that you missed. Sometimes the errors they find are small, but important: an unclear reference, a need to remind the reader who a character is, bad grammar, awkward phrasing. Other times the errors can be bigger: Is this character convincing? Is this scene confusing? Should the end be the beginning? Is there something said so subtly that it's missed? Conversely, is something so overstated that the reader feels beaten about the head by it?

You can learn a lot from what people say about your work. You can also learn a lot from what they say about *other* people's work. So even when it's not "your turn," you're still learning things you can use in your own writing.

It's a real pleasure to hear weekly installments of something you like reading; I enjoy listening to other group members' work as much as I like hearing what they think of my own. (Well, *almost* as much. That, by the way, is another reason why it's so important that you like the writing style of the other members.)

I prize the friendship I find in my writing group as much as the great advice about writing. These days, when everybody has to lug out a fourteen-pound Day-Timer to schedule a lunch (which cannot occur any earlier than a month from now, and then it will probably have to get canceled, anyway), it's good to know I'll be seeing others I care about regularly, with no planning at all.

WHAT ARE THE DANGERS IN A WRITING GROUP?

Well, I'm sorry to have to say this, but it's true: A lot of writers are very jealous people. They're stingy with praise and high-handed with criticism. However unconsciously, they don't want others to succeed because they wrongly believe it will take away from them. People like that have no business in a writing group, but oftentimes they find their way in. And they work on a group like slow poison. What can happen to members in a group with such a writer is that they may feel humiliated and discouraged, even fearful, rather than supported and inspired. And what's really dangerous is that those threatened members often keep their feelings to themselves, thinking no one else feels that way. Ultimately, they can leave the group, when they're not the ones who should leave at all.

Another bad group member is the one who, for any reason, thinks she is entitled to most of the attention. Meeting after meeting, she will make sure that happens—one way or another. There are always times when one writer in a group requires more time than the other members. But it can't be the same writer all the time!

In the way that women living in the same dorm can begin to menstruate together, it may happen that members in a writing group can begin to write things that are similar. If the writers involved are strong, and if they have clear ideas about what they're doing, this can be all right. If such is not the case, you may, however unconsciously, begin to copy—or be copied from. Be aware of this possibility. In the end, if there are too many similarites between writers, one of the writers may need to bring in something else to work on.

Sometimes you get suggestions from group members that may be appropriate for what they've seen so far, but do not fit for what the work is going to become. This is something the author must learn to factor in, when considering criticism of longer pieces of work. Also, remember that when you are reading something out loud, small piece by small piece, with a good length of time separating each of those readings, it's a very different experience than reading a book as a whole. What doesn't work on near-microscopic examination may in fact work well otherwise—when it is in context with the rest of the piece still to come, say, or when it is read quickly with the eye rather than slowly out loud. A writer has to trust her intuition, to be able to say, "Well, this may sound strange now, but trust me, I think it will make sense later." Otherwise, she might abandon terrific ideas whose worth would have been proven later on.

There may come a time, even if you're in with really good people, when you get Group Fatigue. You just all of a sudden need to take some time away from it. Perhaps what the members say in their critiques has begun to seem too predictable. Perhaps your life has temporarily been flooded with other obligations. Or maybe your writer's soul is just asking for more solitude.

If any of this happens, it's probably fine to take a brief leave of absence. Tell the group you need some downtime, and let them know when you expect you'll be able to come back. (And then be sure to be understanding when someone else wants time off later.)

There are some people who feel that writing groups take too much time away from writing. They think rather than sitting around talking about your own work and that of others, you could—and should—be working. In my experience, this happens more often when a group meets in the daytime. When I was in such a group, there were plenty of times I felt stretched, taking time away from writing to go to my group. And on a few occasions, I called and said I couldn't come because I was on a tear—I needed to stay home and keep going on what I was doing. Others in the group did this as well. In a good group, everyone will be tolerant of this happening. But you can't do it too often, because being a member of a group also means that you offer a real commitment to *be* there.

The worst dangers associated with writing groups are that people can take suggestions too literally, or too much to heart. If they take them too literally, they can start feeling crazy. Member X says to do this, Y says to do this, and Z says to do something completely different than both of them! What is a writer to do? Well, what a writer should do is see what, if anything, seems like great advice; what makes sense; what sits right in the gut. And ignore the rest.

Other times, suggestions will be in sync: Everyone will say essentially the same thing. Usually, *but not always,* it behooves a writer to pay attention to opinions so uniform in nature.

If someone takes suggestions too much to heart, she loses control of her own story and starts trying to write to someone else's specifications of what her story should be. This should never, never happen, but it does. If you join a group, you must be ever mindful of the fact that the suggestions you hear are simply that. As a writer, you own your own material.

HOW DO YOU START A GROUP?

As has been mentioned, one of the best places to meet potential group members is in a writing class. Otherwise, you might look for people in organizations like book clubs, or you can advertise. Put an ad in a community paper, or hang up signs in bookstores, libraries, and coffeehouses.

It's best to start small. Five people is plenty. If you get too few, you won't get enough feedback; if you get too many, you won't get enough of your own material read.

A leader usually emerges in a group—someone who will at least keep an eye on time, but also steer the discussion a bit (often by initiating it). The leader will also make the quiet decision that it's time to move on to the next reader.

Expect that it will take three or four meetings for members to begin to feel comfortable in a writing group, even if they knew each other beforehand.

WHAT MAKES FOR A GOOD GROUP MEMBER?

Someone who is committed, first of all. A group can't work if members show up one week, then not the next two. Neither can it work if people aren't willing to stay for the length of time a group meeting requires. Occasionally people have to leave early or come late. But it should be rare that this happens.

A group member should love reading and writing. She should be able to handle criticism of her work without becoming defensive or argumentative. Neither should she be so invested in what she says about another's work that she takes offense if people don't agree with her. Sometimes a group member (or members) seems intent on turning a critiquing session into some sort of contest: Who can make the best suggestion, the most insightful remark? This is not helpful for anyone, especially the writer being critiqued, whose work gets buried under someone else's ego.

A good writing group member should be generous. When something is really good, she should heap praise on it. Also, she should be happy when someone else in the group has success. It's hard not to feel the twist of envy from time to time, especially if you've been having a hard time and someone else is having one great thing after the other happen. You can, in fact, feel envious of others even if things *are* going fine for you. It's like a kid who's just been given a doll, staring at another kid who's just been given the exact same doll. Each kid can't help wondering if that *other* doll isn't just a little bit better.

What's most important about envy, I think, is that you admit to it when it comes, and then do everything you can to get rid of it. Think of it as cockroaches in the kitchen of the soul. They may come. But they're bad, and you have to get rid of them. And then they might come again, and you have to get rid of them again. Remember: Envy hurts most the one who feels it.

The most important thing a writing group member can do is offer consistently thoughtful comments about other people's work, things that let the writer know she has truly paid attention to what has been put before her. If she wears great clothes and perfume, knows how to make crab dip, or has a dog who weighs forty-five pounds or more, it's a big bonus.

HOW CAN YOU TELL IF A WRITING GROUP IS WORKING FOR YOU?

This is sort of like asking how to tell if you're in love. If you have to ask . . .

But: If you are in a good writing group, you will value the suggestions you receive, and they will help you write more, and better. You will learn new things. You will look forward to going to your group, feeling rather like you're going to a little party, as opposed to the OR for necessary but painful abdominal surgery. You will feel a sense of caring and good-

will coming from other members, and you will feel that
toward them as well.

Homework

Talk to at least one person who is in a writing group. Ask
for pros and cons. If you're already sure you'd like to try
being in a group, hang up an ad in an appropriate place, or
ask in a local bookstore if they know of existing groups
looking for new members.

11 *The Business of Writing*

> Editors and readers don't know what they want to
> read until they read it. Besides, they're always
> looking for something new.
> —WILLIAM ZINSSER

If you are interested in being published, you need to know something about the business of writing. This means learning things like how to submit your finished work, and to whom, and what you might expect after doing so. It means communicating effectively with editors and other people in the publishing world, and creating a system to manage your bookkeeping. Most important, though, it means looking at your*self* as a business.

One of the hardest things for unpublished authors to do is to take themselves seriously as writers. In part, that's because it's so rare for *others* to take them seriously. Almost every time I tell people whom I've just met that I'm a writer, I see a barely suppressed smile. *Uh-huh*, I know they're thinking. *Right*. They ask me if I've been published and I say yes. Then they ask what I've published and I say novels. Then they ask my name and who my publisher is. When I tell them, I suddenly pass the worth test, and am no longer the Great Pretender.

If you take away nothing else from this book, please

learn this: Just because you have not been published, it does not mean you're not a writer. It is not signing a contract or taking money for words that makes you a writer. Rather, it is having a certain sensibility, a measure of talent, and a need to express yourself on paper. There's not a doubt in my mind that some extremely fine writing is lying around in someone's desk drawer. Or in a letter they wrote today. Or in their journal. Or, unfortunately, in their garbage can.

If you write, call yourself a writer—to yourself and others— out loud. If you want to be published, make writing a business, and be your own CEO. Then, since you're thinking of yourself as a CEO, act like one:

BUY A LEXUS
Just kidding. Not that there's anything wrong with a Lexus.

HAVE A VISION
Know, as clearly as you can, what your aspirations are, even if you keep them entirely to yourself. Maybe you want to write razzle-dazzle screenplays in Hollywood and take meetings by the pool between parties, massages, and therapy. Maybe you want to pen quiet, literary novels, writing longhand at an old wooden desk, before a tall, curtainless window. Maybe you want to write books that make no demands on the intellect, that just make people laugh or have a good time.

Whatever it is that you want to achieve, honor it as a legitimate goal within yourself first. Then work on it; fan the flames; keep it alive; do not disrepect it.

HIRE THE GOOD; FIRE THE BAD

What I mean by this is that you should try to keep in your life the things and the people who encourage you in your writing, and minimize or eliminate contact with those who discourage you. This sounds as though I think it's simple; in fact, I know it's not.

Suppose, for example, you have a spouse or significant other who, whether he/she means to or not, consistently makes you feel bad about your work. Perhaps after reading your pages, he/she smiles and says nothing, or—worse— offers a response so vague or tactful you feel your stomach descend to your knees. In a situation like this, you've got to learn not to let that person read your work. This is hard to do; most of us want those whom we love best to share in the things that matter to us. But asking for an opinion on your writing makes you so acutely vulnerable, especially when you've just begun work on something. You have to learn to guard the eggs in the nest. If you feel you really want another's opinion, find someone more gentle and encouraging. (A writing group is good to consider.) Don't keep setting yourself up for a fall.

There are times when one partner undermines another's writing even without having seen the work. He or she isn't interested in seeing the work and thinks the notion of wanting to write is silly, a pipe dream, a waste of time, per- haps even an embarrassment. If you are coupled with someone like that, someone who does not encourage you in your passions, who in fact belittles them, ask your partner to go out and get the newspaper, and then quickly change the locks. Especially the one to your heart.

Interestingly enough, there are times when others can actually be too supportive—when their efforts to encourage you backfire. These people ask to see your work too often and too soon, and talk so excitedly about your efforts to you and others that, rather than feeling encouraged, you begin to feel what my friends and I call the worm of shame squirming through your gut, because you *know* it's not *that* good, at least not *yet*. These pathologically supportive people can even unconsciously start trying to take over your work, telling you how to write, how to market what you write, how to feel about what other people say.

Overly supportive people present a very tricky situation. Often, they are people with whom you have a close relationship, and they seemingly are just trying to show you how much they care, how much they are willing to do for you. So you feel guilty for not being grateful. But in a situation like this, there's more than meets the eye. Maybe there's unexpressed jealousy involved; maybe there are control issues; maybe another person is trying to live through you. It really doesn't matter what underlying dynamic is at work: If others' support feels more like pressure, you must break free. Tell them you really appreciate their desire to help you, but you need to keep your work to yourself, at least at first. And tell them you need to keep, well, kind of *quiet* about writing in general.

People who support you in the right way make you feel really good about writing. They give you encouragement without sounding false. They try hard not to be resentful of the time you need to take away from them to write. Also— and this is critical—they make you feel that you will do even better. That's not because they don't like what they're seeing now; rather, it's because they like what they're seeing enough to believe that you're in this for the long haul, and that you will continue to grow and improve as a writer.

You will discover, with time and experience, what things work to keep your writing spirits up versus what things work against you. Then you must consistently be your own advocate in doing what is best for your writing. Again, it is not always easy. It is only always necessary.

PRIORITIZE

Barbara Lazear Ascher is the author of a memoir, *Landscape Without Gravity*, as well as two wonderful collections of essays, *The Habit of Loving* and *Playing After Dark*. She offers this advice to writers: "Say 'No.' Let 'Yes' be the exception. As much as I love my friends, I treat the time when I'm writing a book [which appears to average three years per book] as though I've been sent into solitary confinement. I don't accept luncheon dates or breakfast dates and go out only one night a week. I find that writing requires uninterrupted concentration and physical fitness. So, I get at least half an hour of exercise every day—walking the dog, swimming, going to the gym—to keep strong enough to endure the physical rigors of sitting at a desk—and to clear my brain."

Here is a woman who is clear about putting writing first, and I think it's a good thing to learn, with one exception. When you have young children, and you are the primary caretaker, I think they must come first. If they don't, I think it will hurt both of you. This is *not* to say that you should put your writing aside when you have children; rather, it is to encourage you to work around their schedule as much as you can.

When I began writing for publication, I got a separate phone line for business calls only. I got that phone a long time before I got an answering machine, and so whenever it rang, I answered it. If my children were at home, they knew they were not to interrupt me when I was on that particular line.

I cannot tell you how much I regret making this rule. For one thing, I know now from my own experience that there is nothing wrong with hearing occasional ambient noise when you are having a business conversation. One of the most pleasant things to have happened to me during a telephone interview with a newspaper reporter was that I got to hear the interviewer's two-year-old child in the background. The interviewer was embarrassed; I was thrilled. I wanted to hurry up with the interview and talk to the kid.

The bigger reason I regret making that rule is that I hurt my children. My older daughter, now in her twenties, told me recently how much she used to dread that phone ringing, how it took so much time away from her and made her feel very much a lesser priority. Whether it really took too much time away from her is not the issue; she perceived it that way. There is, after all, a big difference between seeing your parent go off somewhere to work versus having them sit *right in front of you* and yet still be unavailable. It's kid agony. (This is a case for getting an office site away from your house, if you possibly can.)

I'm afraid I'm going to have to tell you what all the grandparents say: Children grow up so fast. Don't shortchange yourself by leaving too little time for them when they are young. Anyway, they're terrific material: I made my living for years writing essays inspired by them.

In order not to cheat yourself, you have to make writing a high priority. You have to make it very nearly sacred. But you have to live the rest of your life, too; you have to allow room for all that makes you you, for all that feeds you. In my mind, being more *than* a writer means you're more *of* a writer.

DEVELOP AND MAINTAIN A GOOD REPUTATION

This means that you hold to a certain level of professionalism in all aspects of your writing business. Let's look at submissions to magazines, for example. Here are the words of Marcia Nelson, assistant to Elizabeth Crow, editor in chief of *Mademoiselle.*

"My best advice for anyone who is interested in submitting an article for publication is to first *read* the periodical you hope to write for. I can't tell you how many times I've opened a submission request, and either the letter has been addressed to the previous editor or the writer has misspelled the current editor's name. This goes in my immediate 'reject' pile. My secondary 'reject' pile includes those submissions for types of work that we have never published, or no longer publish, such as fiction or poetry. Anyone who picks up a current issue of *Mademoiselle* can see that we do not publish anything in either of these two categories."

How about agents? What do they think about? What do they look for? What do they really do? Here are the words of my agent, Lisa Bankoff:

"I became an agent after deciding not to become a lawyer, but even my 'why I want to go to law school' essay was a harbinger. In it, I wrote about my desire to protect the rights and interests of writers who otherwise have little access to or recourse in dealing with the big and increasingly bigger publishing companies. And that, in a nutshell, is precisely the service I offer writers today, plus some.

"A good, thoughtful query letter is an excellent way of getting my attention. It should convey a straightforward sense of the material. In fiction, it's interesting for me to know to whom the author feels his or her book would appeal: say, to readers who enjoy Jane Hamilton or who are fans of John Updike. A short description of the story line and first chapter are usually all I need in order to know whether I'm the right agent for the book. Some agents will ask for a synopsis. I generally find a detailed synopsis to be an absolute bore, a scaffold conveying no sense of the strength or character or depth of beauty of the structure it limns.

"In nonfiction, a proposal is essential. It should contain an overview or introduction to the material, a sample chapter, a projected outline, and information about the author. With nonfiction, you'll want to demonstrate an awareness of other books that may be competitive with yours and be prepared to indicate how your treatment of the subject will distinguish itself from others.

"What *not* to do: Don't spend money and effort on elaborate embossed leather presentation folders. Keep it simple. Don't have unrealistic expectations of getting a response overnight—three to four weeks is more like it. Keep an open mind; if you start to hear a consensus of opinion about what's wrong with your material, it may be time to think and revise. Do *not* write in imitation of some misguided notion of what makes a bestseller. No one knows for sure."

Lisa Dicker is Lisa Bankoff's assistant. She, like most assistants to people in publishing, is a wealth of great information. She read what Lisa Bankoff wrote, then generously added some of her own thoughts:

"I'd really like to emphasize the part about keeping a submission simple—in both content *and* presentation. I've seen manuscripts arrive in boxes that are embedded with flower petals and in one case the pages were actually scented! We all realize that, for most people, a manuscript submission is akin to submitting a piece of the writer's heart, and those pages feel more like a part of the writer's soul, not just a story. But the bottom line is that an agent is looking for something that is sellable, and writers have to realize that sending photos of their family or children or adorable poodle is not going to enhance their material. The writing has to speak for itself.

"As for nonfiction, the most common pitfall I've seen new writers walk into is this: Most 'great ideas for a book' are actually great ideas for a magazine article. Again the keyword here is 'sellable,' and for a lot of nonfiction book ideas (as interesting as they may be), a writer has to be realistic about how much attention a reader can give to certain off-beat topics. Some writers get so excited about their interest that they don't stop to ask themselves the hard question—that is, will people want to read two hundred pages on this topic or will five pages in a magazine do the trick?

"I highly recommend *How to Write a Book Proposal* by Michael Larsen. This is a great book for nonfiction writers just starting out. This is the book I tell my relatives to buy when they approach me after Thanksgiving dinner and whisper that they've always wanted to write a book about . . . but just don't know where to begin."

In addition to taking care with the way you present your material, be mindful of how you present yourself. Marjorie Braman, editor extraordinaire at HarperCollins (and editor of this very book you're reading) describes her version of nightmare writers as "those who are arrogant enough to believe that in addition to writing the book, they know best how to package it, promote it, advertise it, and sell it!" Her ideal writer, on the other hand, "would be outwardly modest, but possess a strong sense of self." Marjorie looks at about twenty-five manuscripts a month and says what matters most to her when she's reading fiction is "a character, or characters, whom I really get involved with emotionally and truly care about." She also says these encouraging words: "It's very competitive, but good books will always find an enthusiastic editor. So if you believe in yourself, don't give up!"

Marjorie Braman's assistant is a man named Jeffery McGraw, who is a writer, too. Here are his thoughts:

"If a writer seeks to get published, the most important thing—and the first step that needs to be taken—is to actually have something to publish. Being a member of an editorial staff, I receive countless letters of inquiry out of the blue from people who have ideas for novels they've yet to write. Only if you are a published author will a major publishing house ever consider agreeing to a contract deal based on an outline alone. Exceptions to this rule might include high-profile celebrity status. Barring this, 'everyday' unpublished authors should expect to submit (or have ready to submit) a completed manuscript.

"Before I got into this world of publishing, I had no idea what *The Literary Market Place* was, but now I find it an invaluable tool as a writer. This huge directory is not just a complete guide to the publishing world, but details what each publishing company specializes in—romances, mysteries, biographies, military books, et cetera. This helps a lot, since you wouldn't want to send, for instance, your erotic thriller to a house whose specialty is ultraconservative religious studies!

"Some people write to me with an avant-garde attitude toward getting published. 'I don't believe in agents,' many of them declare. Many also try to 'challenge' editors to find adequate reasons for rejection. Well, guess what? It won't get you far, at least where I work. Editors and their assistants have no time for such shenanigans. We get enough manuscripts directly from agencies that we are obliged to read through, which leaves little time for concentrating on all of the other aspects of the publishing business—scheduling, editing, attending meetings, et cetera. I've had many people ask what I do all day, thinking I sit comfortably at my desk and read leisurely from nine to five with a lunch break in between. Wrong! Most of us don't have time to read during the day, as we go to meetings to discuss manuscripts we stayed up reading until midnight the night before, or meetings to decide how to market and publicize the books we already have agreed to publish. It's a busy world, and my point is that the conventions of dealing with agents and other industry associates are essential to keeping our 'houses' in order, so to speak.

"That said, most of us love what we do, no matter how much it consumes our lives. And we really take pride in our authors."

Comments from insiders are very helpful for understanding what really goes on in the offices of people who publish. But in the end, common sense and common courtesy are what will take you furthest when trying to establish a good reputation. Therefore: Learn as much as you can about the places where you want to submit your work. Honor your commitments. Do the best job you can with any piece of writing that you do. Maintain a positive and polite attitude with the people in publishing with whom you work. Try to be brief when you're on the phone. Finally, don't burn any bridges; you never know who's going to end up where. For example, a junior member of a magazine staff may end up as its editor in chief. An editor at one magazine will sometimes move to another. The more good relationships you have, the better off you are.

HAVE A STRONG SENSE OF ETHICS

I heard from a writer friend the other day about a writer friend of hers who had decided to use a few of my friend's lines in his book (without crediting her). He thought of it as a tribute. Taking other people's material is not a form of flattery; it is a form of plagiarism.

Be careful, too, about subject matter that makes you or someone else vulnerable or frankly exposed. Oftentimes, someone writes about things as a way of sorting them out, or of coming to terms with them. That's fine. That's good. But be careful about what you publish when a situation is volatile.

Sometimes you know full well that what you write will hurt someone in one way or another, but you feel you have to publish it anyway. And you may be exactly right. Other times you're not sure; there are compelling reasons to go either way. When you're confronted with a situation like the latter, think hard about what you have to lose and what you have to gain by publishing the work. If there's more to lose, let it go. There are other things to write about. And it may happen that a better time (or a better way) to write about it will come along later anyway.

Ideas for Submissions to Magazines

I have sold hundreds of magazine articles. A very few of these were service-oriented. All the rest were personal essays that were inspired mostly by feelings: fear, anger, frustration, sadness, nostalgia, happiness. I'm going to share with you a list of some of the things I wrote about, because the ideas are recyclable, and they may spark an idea for an article in you.

↭ *on disciplining older kids*

↭ *the value of a retreat alone*

- *the bittersweet job of parenting*

- *memories of the first day of school*

- *admiration of a friend going through chemotherapy (seeing how she was still herself)*

- *the importance of praise*

- *a humor piece on the real estate experience*

- *a humor piece on fifteen reasons why women are better than men (Boy, did this get mail!)*

ꙮ ꙮ ꙮ

- *what we leave behind (the sorrows of growing up)*

- *a short story about a kid matchmaking two elderly people*

- *a short story about the reality of divorce*

- *thoughts on Janet Atkins, who died with the assistance of Dr. Kevorkian*

- *a look at the summers of my youth*

◡ *my best Christmas memory*

◡ *in defense of teens*

◡ *marriage: myth versus reality*

◡ *the value of women friends*

◡ *why homemade matters*

◡ *why my grandfather was such an inspiration*

◡ *the bad haircut (lots of mail for this one, too)*

෨ ෨ ෨

◡ *what we do have time for*

◡ *thinking about old boyfriends*

◡ *plastic surgery: What do you gain? What do you lose?*

◡ *getting dressed: mission from hell*

◡ *grocery store blues (everything that can go wrong there)* ᴥ *how parents should behave when they have teens (according to the teens)*

ᴥ *Aunt Lala's meat loaf*

ᴥ *a tribute to the sweeties in my life (on candy)*

ᴥ *a short story about a thief who ends up making the woman he steals from question her marriage*

ᴥ *what parents are doing right*

ᴥ *the worth of blubber*

ᴥ *dates with greats (fantasy piece about dating your idols)*

ᴥ *the ideal doctor*

So there are a few ideas to ponder. On the whole, humor and nostalgia always seem to work the best, at least in terms of reader response.

There are many, many books available that tell you how and where to submit articles. I recommend using *The Writer's Market* (buy it if you can afford it), but don't rely on it alone. Once you've chosen a magazine you'd like to submit to, make sure you have the name and address right. If you're submitting a personal essay or a humor piece, send the entire manuscript. Otherwise, send a proposal with a cover letter. If you have publishing credits, include them in the cover letter. If you do not, you need not advertise that fact, as I did, the first time I sent out a query. "I've never written for magazines," I began. *Please* don't do *that*.

THE WAITING GAME

After you submit your query or manuscript (along with a self-addressed, stamped envelope), you are going to have to wait a while to hear back about your story. It will probably be three to eight weeks, and it will feel like ten years. The best thing to do is to move on to the next piece(s). If you don't hear about your submission after eight weeks, send a follow-up letter. If you still don't hear, you might try a polite phone call.

Once you break into a magazine, it will take less time to hear back on subsequent submissions. You are also more likely to be given assignments that are not on speculation. In these cases, you are asked to write a piece for an agreed-upon amount of money, and you are usually given a kill fee if it ends up not working out. The kill fee is much smaller than what you would have been paid if the piece were accepted, but it does provide some compensation for your time and effort.

There may be times when you'll be asked to change a manuscript if you want it to be accepted. I think when you're first starting to write for publication, you should be pretty open to compromise. Try to do any rewrites yourself, but if you can't, be open to seeing what your editor does. However: If you feel a wall of resistance rise up in your stomach, if you actually feel a little sick at the prospect of doing what's asked, *don't do it*. Stand by your man(uscript). I want to emphasize that this kind of resistance should not happen very often. But when your response to an editing suggestion is so strongly negative, I think you have to respect your feelings about your own work.

Incidentally, in my experience, book editors tend to honor the author's inclination much more readily than magazine editors do.

This is not because of any mean-spiritedness on the part of the magazine editor; rather, it usually reflects the audience/advertiser concerns they have.

Daily Routines

It's always interesting to me how daily routines differ among writers. Isabel Allende says she starts her books on the same January day each year. And each writing day, she lights a candle and writes for the length of time the candle burns. Truman Capote wouldn't write in a room with yellow roses. Elizabeth Searle writes in bed, longhand. Barbara Lazear Ascher works one hour before breakfast. "Straight from dreams is the best time," she says. "Coffee and hot milk only. Then the reward is breakfast and a day of work that seems to go much better. I write until one P.M., break for lunch with my husband, and yes, if you can stand it, then nap with my husband. Trollope was right: Three hours is all a man should write. I keep testing this, but find that after the fourth hour what I write is redundant and ends up on the cutting room floor. So the afternoon is best spent walking in Central Park and trying to assimilate what I've written and what I want to write the next day, or editing, or reading physics, which for whatever reason soothes me. Probably because it all seems so wonderful and I can't understand a word of what I read.

"I wish I had a Zen desk. Perfectly designed emptiness. Instead I have a clutter of pictures of Venice, the Pantheon in Rome, Van Eyck's painting *The Mystic Lamb,* and whatever poem I'm loving at the moment. None of this is required, but I think they help remind me that what I'm doing is pretty darn small in the scheme of things. The only thing I *need* nearby is my dog, who lies at my feet. There's something about his sighs and his twitches in sleep that soothe me. Writing, for me, is a terrifying act."

I find a twenty-minute snooze in the middle of the day remarkably restorative. Jane Hamilton, author of three very fine novels, *The Book of Ruth, A Map of the World,* and *The Short History of a Prince,* agrees. "I have a couch in my study because taking a nap is critical to the creative process. I usually let myself sleep for half an hour in the middle of the day. This is the perk of being self-employed."

Amy Bloom, author of *Come to Me,* a collection of short stories that was nominated for a National Book Award (and that will take your breath away), as well as *Love Invents Us,* a terrific novel, says this about her writing routine:

"I am only eccentric in my spectacular powers of procrastination, which are adolescent in their intensity and middle-aged in their durability. I will garden, make coffee, check for mail, read the *Times,* call the regulars, and reread an entire Elizabeth George novel before I get down to writing fiction.

I would love to have flowers and order—however, I write amid piles of paper on the floor, teapots full of pens, clocks that don't work, and photographs of my children when they were much, much younger. The only thing I really rely on is a door that closes and my computer. In a pinch, a door that closes and a pad and a pen. I also very much like to have my Henry James quote, 'We work in the dark. We do what we can. We give what we have.' Nearby, a few of the birthday cards my kids have made over the years, and a couple of dear and peculiar Limoges boxes. My only literary stimulants are other people's fine poetry and deadlines."

This is all very interesting, but what's important is for you to understand that you must develop and adhere to your own routine. There is no magic. Well, there *is* magic, but you must create your own. Your ways of writing have to be as unique as you are.

A Suggestion for a Bookkeeping System

I am a person who freezes like a deer in the headlights when the checkout person at the grocery store says, "Want to give me seven cents and I'll give you back a dollar?" So I am the last person to talk about a bookkeeping system. Nonetheless, just in case it might help you, I want to share with you a system I used for many years that helped me keep track of article submissions and sales.

Each time I sent off a manuscript, I wrote the title on an index card. Beneath that, I wrote the magazine I sent it to and the date I sent it. If it was accepted, I noted that and the date; if it was rejected, I noted that date as well, then listed the next market I sent it to. Editors will tell you that pieces sent to them must be tailored specifically to their unique needs, and to some extent they are right. But there is enough of an overlap among some magazines that you can send the exact same piece to several markets. This is especially true for humor or personal experience pieces. Often, in fact, I would make a list of potential markets on the index card before I ever sent the piece out. Then, when it came back from one place, I just sent it right back out again, to the next name on the list.

Sometimes I sold a piece to the first place I sent it to. Sometimes I sold it after sending it to two or three places. If I didn't sell a piece after sending it to four places, I usually retired it, at least for the time being. But if I really believed in a piece, I'd keep on sending it out. (One piece got sent out seventeen times before it was taken. Which was fine, because by the time the thing got taken, my rates had gone up. That piece, by the way, generated a lot of positive reader mail.)

I tried to keep in circulation as many pieces as I could. Because I write quickly, and often, I usually had about ten manuscripts out at any given time. The index cards helped me keep track of how much longer I might have to wait to hear about a piece, and when I should follow up on something that was taking too long. (Usually, the longer you wait, the better; but this is not always true. Also, you usually hear by phone about an acceptance, by mail about a rejection.)

When I sold something, I noted the date, the name of the article, the magazine it sold to, and the amount of money I was due in a separate notebook, with columns set up to accommodate that information. This way, I knew at a glance what income was coming in, and how much I should reasonably spend on winter coats. When I received the check, I noted the date I received it; and when the piece ran in the magazine, I noted that date as well.

If you work hard at it, you can sell a lot of articles. The highest number of articles I sold in one month was seven; in a year, thirty-seven. There was one happy day (July 13, 1989, as a matter of fact) when I got three acceptances. (In the previous month, however, I had sold nothing.)

Dealing with Rejections

Over and over again, you hear stories about very famous people who suffered all kinds of rejections. Those stories never did much for me. Neither did stories of people who kept all their rejection slips. Rejection slips that have encouraging messages might be worth keeping; otherwise, get rid of them.

I think the best way to deal with rejection is to make sure your life is about more than writing. It's critical to keep a balance in your life of a mix of things, to have friends or family or hobbies or another job, or all of this, to offset the intensity of writing for publication.

It's also critical to keep some perspective. The best training I got for dealing with rejection came from having been a nurse. When you've cared for people in truly dire circumstances, when you've seen close up how suddenly cruel and arbitrary life can be, a rejection slip or a bad review doesn't seem like such a big deal.

Understand, too, that things get rejected for a lot of reasons. Your writing may be wonderful—it may be your timing, your subject, or an editor's quirks that get between you and a sale. Try to find your richest joy and satisfaction in the writing itself. Let the rest be gravy. Good gravy, but gravy.

Dealing with Success

This is a good problem, right? Well, not to the person who is having it.

Success can do funny things: It can make you feel guilty, make you feel phony, make you anxious about your next work. But the worst thing that happened to me as a result of success is that I lost my best friend, Phyllis Florin. I got her back, but not without enormous psychic cost to both of us.

I am the kind of person who cannot enjoy something fully unless I share it. And so I wanted my best friend, the one who encouraged me to be a writer, involved in all the wonderful things that happened to me as a result of having become one. At first, she was happy for me. Then I began to feel her hostility. And then we fell apart.

Envy is such an important, painful, and widespread issue, I asked Phyllis to write about it for this book. Here is how she describes what happened to us:

Envy is such a degrading thing to have to own up to. Who wants to admit to being so black in soul, so low in character that you can't be happy for your best friend? It was as hard for me to understand as anyone else—why I couldn't embrace my friend's good fortune, why I couldn't be there for her with a generous and open heart. I certainly didn't want the part of the ugly stepsister.

Envy is a dark tangled web of deprivation, greed, desire, abandonment, loss, despair, and fear. It's all the things we think we have packed away in the basement. I tried for a very long time to sort through everything that happened to Beth and me. I wanted to make neat orderly piles—that over there, this over here. It was impossible. I thought, for instance, that I was envious because I was a poor kid who always had her nose pressed up against the rich kid's window, but I have rich friends who wrestle with envy just as much as I do, so it's not just because of that.

And then I thought I was the "jealous type," insecure, with low self-esteem, but now I don't think there is a type. I think we all have envy buttons, it's just a matter of what and who pushes them. Aeschylus said a long time ago, "It is in the character of very few men to honor without envy a friend who has prospered."

Even though Beth and I have survived the worst of it (and I hope that was the worst of it), it's not gone. It slithers around in the dark. We can be talking on the phone and she'll casually mention something about her latest book and there it is, the coiled rattlesnake. Not like it used to be, but there.

It was a happy time for both of us when she was first published. We were going to be rich! Famous! I was like Barney Fife, adjusting the waist of my pants, "Yah, I'm her friend," I sniffed.

I could see the two of us at some chic place like 21, with hats low over our eyes, red lips and fingernails, sipping martinis. She'd be signing autographs and I'd be beaming beside her, her trusted friend, her Thelma Ritter, offering wisecracks and wisdom, keeping her balanced, down-to-earth.

It was a pleasure to read everything she wrote. I was amazed, sometimes astounded, by her talent. I still am, by the way. If I had discovered Elizabeth Berg on my own, I would have done anything to meet her, and would have envied the woman who was lucky enough to be her best friend.

It didn't come completely out of the blue, the thing that turned me dark side out. I had been jealous of Beth before. When we were younger, I sometimes felt jealous of her looks. I hated how men's eyes would flit past me to her. Later, she got married and had babies when I was barely holding on, living in a residence club in San Francisco with wackos and creeps on disability. I felt she had violated the clause in our friendship contract that prohibited one from being happy when the other was miserable.

The writing success, though, was more than I could handle. After she'd been published more times than I thought necessary, every time the phone rang, I reacted as though a gun had gone off. Was it Her? It would take every ounce of my actress ability, and I have a certain talent for it, to play the part of the happy, supportive friend. After conversations with her, I'd practically stagger to the bed and lie down, I felt so withered up inside, so exhaus-

ted from pretending. It was as hard work as I've ever
done.

There were days during that dark period when I could
be generous, when the devil was on a coffee break. Days
when I could see my old friend Beth and love her again.
I'd feel so bad for her then that she had to have me as
her rotten friend. But then there were the days when I
saw her only as lording over me, her black cape spread,
her long bony finger with its sharp red nail pointing at
me, cackling: You'll never have what I have. Never never
never.

It became unbearable when *Talk Before Sleep* got on
the *New York Times* bestseller list. I was visiting her at the
time and she showed me (flaunted, I thought) a T-shirt
she had done up with the bestseller list silk-screened on
it. Anyone who's ever been there knows exactly what it
feels like—the big smile plastered on your face and all the
while you're aching and seething with envy; all you want
to do is scream, *So what?* Who cares about the fucking
New York Times?

And then you think, *What if I got on the bestseller list?
Wouldn't I want everyone to know, too?* And then you feel
like shit. You just want out.

It didn't matter, by the way, that her success didn't
change the unhappiness in her life, and it didn't matter
that she coveted many of the things I had. It didn't matter if I counted all my blessings or counted all her flaws.
The comparing was the thing. I never should have been
comparing.

"The flame burns upward, the lake seeps downward."

Number 38, Opposition: The Clinging over the Joyous. The I Ching said, ". . . although the two daughters live in the same house, they belong to different men . . . "

I asked for a sabbatical from the friendship. I felt I had to put some distance between us to find out what was going on. The more I was around her, the more I disliked her, and I didn't want to dislike her. Well, the sane part of me didn't want to dislike her, the envious part loved it. There was a definite pleasure in withholding my friendship.

After we broke up, and it was inevitable, I put it out to the Universe. "Help," I said. "S.O.S." I talked about it to whomever would listen. I wrote down every ugly feeling I had, why I felt inferior to her, and why I shouldn't. I made up conversations between us. One night, hoping I'd gain some fresh insight into it, I told the whole story of us to my husband, from the night we met in 1967 and fell in instant like until we slammed down the phone screaming "fuck you" in 1995.

We did not speak for five months, but a waking hour (and some sleeping) did not go by when I did not think of us, and I swear that's true. Instead of being free of her, she moved in with me. I rewound and replayed every conversation we'd had, what she said, what I said. And then I'd go back and start over, turning over every stone.

I underlined this text in the I Ching in gold pen: "A man misjudges his best friends, taking them to be as . . . dangerous as a wagon full of devils . . . But in the end, realizing his mistake, he lays aside the bow, perceiving that the other is approaching with the best intentions for the purpose of close union."

I have two images of what was going on during that process. One is of ice breaking up. Big chunks of ice breaking free and floating away. The other is of a big wheel, like a wooden mill wheel, starting up after a long rest, creaking and groaning, pulling on the ropes and finally turning again, working.

I was pulling myself away from her.

What I finally understood, in the T. S. Eliot way of returning to the place you started and knowing it for the first time, was that Beth and I are two different people. For the longest time, it had just been the two of us in our little foxhole. We were hunkered down in there playing house, chattering away while the world raged above us. We think so much the same way, share so many memories, that I often wonder if I feel the way I do about certain things because she feels that way, or if it's me.

Two years after we got back together, she sent me a copy of *Joy School*. I had read it in draft form so I thought I'd just scan it, but I got hooked and read the whole book from beginning to end. When I finished, I started crying, way out of proportion to the ending of the book, and then sobbing. I cried because I realized I knew the woman who wrote that book. I knew her well. She was my friend and I loved her.

And then it dawned on me, and I love that expression, because that's exactly what it was like, like the sun coming up over the black horizon, looming big and golden. It dawned on me that we are not the same. I felt the full meaning of the I Ching text: Even though we live in the same house, we are two different people. It was like waking from a bad dream and realizing that everything is all right. I hadn't lost my friend, she was still here. We both are.

For my part, I want to say this:

I *only* had that T-shirt made up to wear to my writing group!! It was how I "told" them about the list! I *never* wore it otherwise, except to *sleep* in!

Seriously, though, some of the worst pain in my life came from feeling like I'd lost Phyllis because I had "too much" success. I know now that I asked too much of her: I wanted her to be not only my best friend, but my husband, my mother, my confessor. I wanted her to be the one person where I put *every*thing. That's a burden no one can bear.

I had a lot of bad feelings about Phyllis and me when all this was happening, and those feelings made for an erosion of the spirit. I suffered mightily because of her jealousy. I also gained a great deal because of her honesty.

I have felt envy, too. And I have seen how it tries to disguise itself, how quickly one can justify one's feeling by denying that it *is* envy. For the most part, though, I feel the world is large enough to accommodate many, many more writers. I feel happy when friends of mine have success. I'm interested in helping people I know and people I don't know, too; that's why I wrote this book. I believe the more good writers we have, the happier we readers will be.

However, I had a lot of good things happen to me fast, and I didn't know any other writers when I began to publish. So I didn't have to hear success stories when I was struggling to be published. I didn't, in fact, really struggle at all. I mean to say that I had a decent-size portion on my plate when I first sat down at the table. Would it have been different if I hadn't already enjoyed some success when I got seriously into the writing business? Would it have been different if Phyllis had had great success before I did? I like to think not, but the truth is, I don't really know. I do know that you don't invite envy. It just comes. And when it does come, you have to learn to deal with it in as fair and honest—and kind—a way as possible.

My priorities about writing feel very clear. I love it; I have done it all my life and I will continue to do it for as long as I can. But I love my relationships with the important people in my life more. I honestly believe I would sacrifice writing success (not writing, but the success) in order to have my lover and my best friend in my life. Luckily, it turns out I don't have to. I am grateful to Phyllis for the extraordinary effort she put forth in order for that to be true. And I am grateful to the man in my life for never resenting my success at all, for encouraging and sustaining me in every way.

Homework

Using various books available to you at stores or in the library, research some markets that you think might be right for you.

If you're considering magazines, read at least five of the most recent issues of all those periodicals to which you might submit. Then make a list of three places you'd start with to send things to. Make sure (by calling the magazine or at least by checking the most recent masthead) that you have the right names and addresses.

If you're considering book publishers, look at at least ten books each company has published. Then, if you feel ready to submit something to a publisher, read about agents. Make a list of five names to send a proposal and/or sample chapter to.

> I'm lying in bed reading a novel. I hear a voice. I
> believe it's coming from the Whitman's box I keep
> in the bottom drawer of my bedside stand. Natu-
> rally I have to open the box. One would be irre-
> sponsible not to find out where a voice in a drawer
> was coming from. Especially in one's own house.
> —ELIZABETH BERG, FROM "DIARY OF A LOSER"

I have yet to write a book where food doesn't figure in, in some way or another. As far as where it fits in a book like this, well, let's just say that food is a wonderful way to reward yourself when you've done a good day's work. It's also important to nourish yourself *while* you're working.

When I first thought about putting recipes in this book, I envisioned finger foods, something that would let you type with one hand and eat with the other. But there's something pretty fine about holding a big bowl of spaghetti on your lap while scrolling down the computer screen. So these recipes are simply ten of my favorites out of a *huge* collection. They are almost all fattening. Most of them are not good for you. Which is why they taste so swell.

This recipe comes from the Black Dog Café on Martha's Vineyard. The first time I made it, I brought it to my writing group, thank God, because otherwise I would have eaten the whole thing. If you make it, bring it somewhere where there are a lot of people who will fall on it like a lover in a romance novel. You don't want any leftovers, because you will suck them down in the car on the way home.

Blueberry Butter Cake

CAKE

    1 cup sugar
    1 tablespoon baking powder
    ½ teaspoon baking soda
    ½ teaspoon salt
    2 ¾ cups flour
    3 eggs, beaten
    1 cup buttermilk
    1 cup melted butter
    1 tablespoon pure vanilla
    3 cups blueberries

TOPPING

    ½ cup sugar
    ¼ cup flour
    ¼ cup cold butter in bits
    cinnamon

Sift together the dry ingredients and in a separate bowl mix the wet ingredients. Then add the wet to the dry and mix until blended. Pour this mixture into a greased and floured 9 × 13–inch pan. Sprinkle with blueberries. In a separate bowl, with your hands, crumble together sugar, flour, butter, and cinnamon for the topping. Sprinkle the topping evenly. Bake at 350 degrees until knife comes out clean, approximately 50 minutes.

Yield: Serves 8 to 10

A nurse with whom I worked many years ago gave this recipe to me. We were sitting around the conference table one evening, having a rare coffee break, and she whipped out a Tupperware container. In it was something that looked delicious and tasted even better. I asked for the recipe and she quickly dictated it. I wrote it on a paper towel, which I still have. This is exactly how that recipe reads.

Or. Pie ("Or" stands for orange. We were in a hurry.)

Melt ½ pound marshmallows and ½ cup milk, stirring only once.

Let cool.

Add 1 cup o.j. and 1 T lemon juice.

Stir in.

Let get very cold—put outside. (This recipe was given to me in Minnesota, in the winter. But a refrigerator, of course, will work just fine.)

Whip ½ cup cream. Fold into mixture. Pour into:

CRUST

1 cup vanilla wafers, crushed
¼ c. butter
⅓ c. sugar
1 t. cinnamon

NOTE: I personally do not like cinnamon in this recipe. It always feels like a pushy guest who shows up uninvited at your carefully orchestrated dinner party, forcing you to get out a dumb folding chair. I leave the cinnamon out.

Yield: Serves 8

And now, so that you don't think all I eat is buttery desserts, I'm going to give you a recipe for a buttery main dish.

People who eat this really feel like lying down and pounding their fists on the floor in ecstasy, but usually they don't. They just eat another helping. Or three.

This recipe is from Molly O'Neill's *New York Cookbook*, probably the only cookbook anybody needs.

Nora Ephron's Sauce Segretto

½ pound (2 sticks) butter (!!!!!! Isn't it *wonderful*????)
1 onion, diced
1 carrot, diced
1 rib celery, diced
1 can peeled tomatoes
½ teaspoon salt
¼ teaspoon freshly ground pepper
¼ to ½ teaspoon dried red pepper flakes
1 pound spaghetti
About ½ cup freshly grated Parmesan cheese

In a nonreactive large sauté pan, melt 1 stick of the butter over medium heat. Add the onion, carrot, and celery, and cook until the onion is translucent but not browned, about 10 minutes.

Dump the can of tomatoes into the pan and mash with a spoon. Cook over medium-low heat until the sauce starts to thicken slightly and picks up the slightly orange color of the carrots, about 30 to 40 minutes.

Cut the remaining stick of butter into slices and stir it into the sauce. Season with salt, pepper, and the dried red pepper flakes—the more red pepper the better.

Meanwhile, cook the spaghetti in boiling, salted water until tender, then drain.

In a large bowl, toss the cooked spaghetti with the sauce. Add the Parmesan cheese and toss before serving.

One hospital where I worked as a nurse put out a newsletter. Once, it proudly noted that the *Minneapolis Star Tribune* had requested the dietary department's recipe for goulash. It is one of my very favorite things—I'll make this huge amount and then happily eat it every day until it's gone.

Fairview Southdale Hospital's Goulash

1 ½ cups ground beef
1 small onion, minced
¼ cup green pepper
1 10-ounce package of egg noodles
½ cup tomato paste
¾ cup tomato sauce
1 medium-size can whole kernel corn, drained
2 teaspoons salt
1 ½ cups catsup
1 ¼ cups tomato juice
½ cup American cheese
½ cup Cheddar cheese

Brown ground beef, onion, and green pepper in frying pan. Drain well.

Cook noodles in boiling salted water until done. Wash in cold water.

Combine meat mixture, noodles, tomato paste, tomato sauce, corn, salt, and catsup.

Add tomato juice to make a juicy consistency.

Pour into pans.

Grate both cheeses and mix together. Sprinkle over casserole.

Bake at 300 degrees for 1 hour.

Yield: Serves 12, unless you have friends like mine, in which case it serves 3.

One of the perks of working at home is that I can make bread. This is my favorite recipe for whole wheat bread, given to me by a real hippie when I was a fake one. Oh, it's worth it to make bread, because it smells so good when it's baking. It's highly therapeutic, too—all that kneading, and that satisfying sense of having made with your own two hands something so earthy and essential. Eat this with butter and jam as soon as it's cool enough to cut. It makes great sandwich bread, too. And toast.

Honey Whole Wheat Bread

2 packages of active dry yeast
½ cup warm water
⅓ cup honey
1 tablespoon salt
¼ cup shortening
1 ¾ cups warm water
3 cups whole wheat flour
3–4 cups all purpose flour
softened butter

Dissolve yeast in ½ cup water. Stir in honey, salt, shortening, 1 ¾ cup warm water, and whole wheat flour. Beat until smooth. Stir in enough flour to make the dough easy to handle. Knead dough until smooth. Place in greased bowl and let rise 1 hour or until volume doubles. Punch down dough, knead again until smooth. Divide dough and place in two 9-inch pans. Brush with butter. Let rise 1 hour. Bake 40 to 45 minutes at 375 degrees. Sniff the air often and sigh with contentment. Bread is done when golden and when it sounds hollow when you tap smartly with one finger on the top of it.

Yield: 2 loaves

When I have the time, I listen to a call-in recipe show called *The Yankee Kitchen*. That's where I got this terrific and really simple recipe, wonderful for Sunday mornings. Also for Monday through Saturday mornings.

Baked Apple Pancake

    1 cup milk
    3 tablespoons sugar
    2 eggs
    ½ teaspoon salt
    ⅔ cup flour
    ½ teaspoon lemon zest
    2 tablespoons butter, melted

Place all ingredients except butter in blender. Process on high.

Melt butter in 9-inch pie plate. Pour in batter, and bake at 400 degrees for 30 to 35 minutes or until a deep golden color and puffed.

TOPPING
    2 tablespoons butter
    2 cups apples, peeled and thickly sliced
    3 tablespoons sugar
    ½ teaspoon cinnamon

Melt butter in skillet. Add remaining ingredients. Cook on medium-low heat until tender. Put onto center of pancake and serve immediately.

This is also good with peaches, plums, nectarines, strawberries, etc.

Yield: Serves 4

This is a little bit of a pain to make, but man oh man, is it worth it. I make it for my daughter Julie all the time because she loves it, too. It came from *First* magazine, which always has great recipes. This is classic Indian. Serve it with Basmati rice.

Chicken in Yogurt Tomato Sauce

3 pounds boneless chicken breasts
2 tablespoons slivered almonds, plus additional toasted almonds for garnish
½ teaspoon fennel seeds
4 cloves garlic
3 tablespoons chopped fresh ginger
3/4 pound tomatoes (about 3)
1 cup yogurt
¼ cup vegetable oil
1 ¼ teaspoons nutmeg
1 teaspoon cardamom, optional
1 teaspoon cumin
1 teaspoon coriander
2 teaspoons salt
½ cup heavy cream
1 ½ teaspoons coarsely grated pepper
⅓ cup chopped fresh coriander, optional

Cut chicken into approximately 1 ½-inch chunks. In a food processor or blender, grind the 2 table- spoons almonds and the ½ teapoon fennel seeds. Set aside. Combine garlic, ginger, tomatoes, and yogurt in a food processor or blender and purée until smooth. Put the tomato mixture and the oil in a large heavy frying pan, and cook over medium-high heat, stirring frequently, until thickened, about 15 minutes. Add chicken and cook until it loses its pink color, about 5 minutes. Do not let chicken brown. Stir in nutmeg, the ground almonds and fennel seeds, cardamom (if using—I do), cumin, ground coriander, and 2 teaspoons salt. Reduce heat and simmer until chicken is just done, about 10 minutes. Stir in cream and pepper. Remove from heat and cover. When ready to serve, reheat, taste for seasoning, and add salt and pepper if needed. Stir in fresh coriander. Garnish with toasted almonds, if desired.

Yield: Serves 6

Well, if a book by me must have recipes, one of the recipes must be for meat loaf. Of my *many* recipes for meat loaf, this is my all-time favorite. It comes from *Family Circle* magazine.

Potato-Frosted Meat Loaf

2 pounds of meat loaf mixture (beef, veal, and pork), or all beef
½ cup canned beef broth
⅓ cup catsup
2 eggs
1 cup packaged Italian-seasoned bread crumbs
½ cup minced celery
1 tablespoon instant minced onion
3 tablespoons finely chopped parsley
1 ½ teaspoons salt
½ teaspoon pepper
2 cups hot seasoned mashed potatoes
⅓ cup grated Parmesan cheese
2 tablespoons butter, melted

Combine meat, broth, catsup, eggs, bread crumbs, celery, onion, parsley, salt, and pepper in a large bowl; mix well. Press mixture into a lightly greased 6-cup mold, or a 9 × 5 × 3–inch loaf pan.

Bake at 350 degrees for 1 hour or until loaf shrinks from the side of the pan. Remove from oven; pour off drippings. Unmold onto cookie sheet.

Combine mashed potatoes with cheese in a medium-size bowl. Frost meatloaf with mixture. Brush potatoes with melted butter.

Bake in a 400-degree oven for 20 minutes, or until potato topping is golden.

Yield: Serves 6

Just to show you I've got some class, here's a recipe for salmon. No butter in it. So be sure to accompany it with rolls and butter. This is from *Bon Appétit* magazine.

Molasses-Glazed Salmon on Mixed Greens with Black Mustard

DRESSING
> 2 tablespoons black mustard seeds
> ¼ cup malt vinegar
> 3 tablespoons honey
> 1 tablespoon dark molasses
> 1 tablespoon golden brown sugar
> ¾ cup vegetable oil
> salt and pepper

SALMON
> ½ cup dark molasses
> ¼ cup Dijon mustard
> 2 tablespoons malt vinegar
> 1 ½ teaspoons chopped shallots
> 1 garlic clove, minced
> ½ teaspoon ground pepper
> 6 7-ounce salmon fillets
> salt and pepper

8 cups mixed greens

For dressing, grind 1 tablespoon mustard seeds to powder. Transfer to small bowl. Add remaining 1 tablespoon mustard seeds and vinegar, honey, molasses, and brown sugar. Whisk well to blend. Gradually whisk in the vegetable oil. Season to taste with salt and pepper.

For the salmon: Mix molasses, mustard, vinegar, shallots, garlic, and pepper in a medium-size bowl. Transfer to a 9 × 13 × 2–inch glass baking dish. Add salmon fillets and turn to coat. Cover and refrigerate 4 hours, turning occasionally.

Preheat broiler. Remove salmon from marinade and discard marinade. Season salmon lightly with salt and pepper. Broil until cooked through, about 5 minutes per side. Transfer salmon to platter. Tent with aluminum foil to keep warm.

Place greens in large bowl. Toss with enough dressing to coat. Divide greens equally among 6 plates. Top with grilled salmon. Drizzle remaining dressing over salmon and serve.

Yield: Serves 6

And now, the grand finale. My favorite recipe for chocolate cake. It's from *Parents* magazine. When I began my tour for *Range of Motion*, I made this cake to bring to a bookstore where I was doing a reading, but I really botched up one side of it. Nobody cared. It was gone in forty-three seconds. You can serve it with a strawberry sitting coyly at one side, or you can be a real swine and eat it with ice cream—soft-serve vanilla, of course. Maybe with some caramel sauce over all. Yum.

Wickedly Delicious Chocolate Cake

1 ¾ cups flour
2 cups sugar
¾ cup unsweetened cocoa powder
2 teaspoons baking soda
1 teaspoon baking powder
1 teaspoon salt
2 eggs
1 cup strong black coffee
1 cup buttermilk
½ cup salad oil
1 teaspoon vanilla

Preheat oven to 350 degrees.

Combine flour, sugar, cocoa, baking soda, baking powder, and salt in the large bowl of an electric mixer. Add eggs, coffee, buttermilk, oil, and vanilla. Beat 2 minutes at medium speed. Batter will be quite thin.

Divide batter between two well-greased and floured 9-inch layer-cake pans. Because this cake is so moist, it's not always easy to remove from the pan. Be sure to grease and flour the pans thoroughly, or bake in a 9 × 13–inch pan.

Bake for 35 to 40 minutes, or until a wooden pick inserted in the center of each layer comes out clean, and cakes are just beginning to pull away from the sides of the pans.

Cool in pans on wire racks for 10 minutes. Remove from pans to cool completely.

Yield: Serves 6

Now, none of these recipes will necessarily make you write better. But they might. Better eat them and find out.

13 Last Lines

> I think a life of wishes, once we are adults, is no life
> at all. It is one thing, as children, when we are
> powerless, to turn to stars and wishbones and can-
> dles on a cake to make our dreams come true. But
> as adults, we need none of that. We can take
> charge of our dreams—if we dare.
> —BARBARA LAZEAR ASCHER
> "ON PASSION," IN *THE HABIT OF LOVING*

After announcing to everyone, from my agent to the mailman, that *this* morning I was going to sit *right* down and *finish this book*, I didn't do it at all. Oh, I sat down at my desk
first thing this morning. But then got I up. I looked at the
newspaper. I threw in a load of towels. And when I passed
the sewing machine on the way back from the washing
machine, I decided to sew for a while. I put together a
square for the quilt I'm working on. Came out nicely.

I played with the dog. I hung a picture back up on a
newly painted wall. I vacuumed the stairs and all of the
upstairs. I inspected the tulips in the backyard: all in excellent health. Vibrant.

Then I got in the car and went over to Pier One and ex-
changed some cushions. Then I went to a café and had a
nice sesame chicken salad for lunch, even though what I
really wanted was a Quarter Pounder with cheese. And then
I went and looked at books, and two hours flew by like a
minute.

You would think I'd get enough of books. They are stacked all over my house. More arrive every week, one way or another. But, like any true book lover, I never do get enough. I regard the shelves in any bookstore with the same mix of lust and longing I experience when I stare into a bakery showcase. Or at Gregory Peck—I don't care how old he is.

I think the reason I procrastinated so much today is that I'm reluctant to say good-bye. I feel like a parent who is having great difficulty leaving her child, and has to keep telling the baby-sitter one more thing.

But the truth is, there's not much more to say. This book is all I know about writing.

So let me just add this.

The other day, I walked to the post office. On the sidewalk outside, an older woman, about seventy-five or eighty, stood reading a paperback book. I walked right past her, very close to her, but I doubt she even saw me, because she was so engrossed. I don't know if she had just received that book in the mail, or if she was killing time waiting for someone, or if it was simply her odd custom to read standing outside the post office. I know only that her pleasure was nearly palpable, and her concentration unbreakable.

Walking farther into town, I passed a young woman and a little girl coming out of the library. The woman had a few books in the crook of one arm, and the little girl clutched a tattered copy of *Alice in Wonderland* to her chest. They were both staring straight ahead and smiling. I thought, *I know how they feel. They can't wait to get home and dive into their treasures.*

What better thing is there than to be part of a process that brings such delight to so many? People of all ages and temperaments love reading, love crawling under the covers, turning on the bedside light, and opening to the place where they left off. Think of it: grandmothers in their nighties, handsome young men wearing tortoiseshell glasses, teenage girls with fluorescent-colored braces, couples who break a rich silence to read passages aloud to each other, convicts who can at least escape in this way—all these people find solace and joy in the pages of a book. Also priests. Bookies. Photographers. Engineers. Cowgirls. Astronauts. Drycleaner clerks. *Some*body from *every*where loves reading. And it's writers who give them the gift of this deeply felt pleasure.

You don't have to write for the public, of course. You can write for your children, for other family or friends, or for yourself alone. But if you bought and read this book, it's because you have a real desire to write. And now it's time to do it.

It is all-fulfilling for me to be a published writer. It is literally a dream come true. I got into this business with no contacts, no writing classes or degree, and no experience. Please believe me when I tell you that with a little talent and perseverance, you can, too. There's only one person who can stop you, and we both know who that is.

If you let yourself answer your own call to write, I hope you, too, experience the profound happiness I have found in doing so. It's the kind of joy that made me once say, in a speech about writing, "I'm not here when I write. I'm there. I like it there very much. I think it's like heaven." And it makes me agree wholeheartedly with P. L. Travers, who said, "If there's a life after death, I want to work."

Homework

If you want to write for publication, spend time today polishing something you wrote. Then, tomorrow, send it out. And then get busy on the next piece.

If you want to write only for yourself, put this book down and pick your pen up.

You're ready.

Go.

THE BEGINNING.

P.S.

Insights,
Interviews
& More . . .

Meet Elizabeth Berg

ELIZABETH BERG BEGAN WRITING at a very early age but waited until 1985, when she was in her thirties, to begin submitting work for publication. Since then, she has published hundreds of magazine articles, nineteen novels, two collections of short stories, and two works of nonfiction. She adapted her novel *The Pull of the Moon* into a play, and co-authored a screenplay based on her novel *Never Change*. Both *Durable Goods* and *Joy School* were selected as ALA Best Books of the Year, *Open House* was an Oprah's Book Club pick, and she received the New England Book Award for her body of

Curt Richter

work. Her books have been published in twenty-seven countries, and three of her novels have been made into television movies. She lives outside Chicago, where she is completing her next novel. She occasionally teaches writing workshops in Positano, Italy, and in selected cities in the United States. ∾

A Few More Exercises

ONE OF MOST IMPORTANT THINGS to
pay attention to in writing is the use
of detail, which helps you avoid *telling*
in favor of *showing*. In my writing
workshops, I focus on three things:
character, place, and dialogue. Here
is a small sample.

Character

Examine a face, even your own, from
the top of the head to the bottom of
the neck. Move down slowly, taking
in as much as you can, noticing how
the features can reveal so much. Here
are a few things you might ask
yourself. . . .

Is the hair nicely groomed or wild
about the head? Is there baldness, and
if so, is it accepted or disguised? Is the
forehead smooth? Freckled? Wrinkled?
Are the eyebrows raised? Furrowed?
Lowered? Over-plucked? So full they
grow horizontally off the face? How
about the eyes: shifty, calm, dazed,
flat? Are the eyelashes long, short,
fake, absent? Noses are all so different
from each other. What distinguishes
the one you're looking at? Is it tiny?
Roman? Broken? The mouth:
Symmetrical? Smiling? Frowning?
Lips full or thin? Cheeks: Dimpled?
Full? Enhanced by high cheekbones?
Pierced? Teeth: Too white? Chattering?
Missing? The chin: Recessed? Doubled?
Does it have a cleft? How is it held:
down, high? The neck: Youthful or
aged? Long or short? Prominent ▶

Adam's apple? Consider the complexion: Pale? Tanning-salon orange? Flushed? Are there tics or compulsions such as constant lip-licking?

After you've made this close study of a face, try these exercises:

- Using the face only, write a description of fear. Rage. Doubt. Love. Confusion. Boredom.

- Now write the way the face changes as the emotion does. For example, write fear becoming replaced by rage, doubt being replaced by love.

Place

Place can often serve as another character in your story. It can also be the thing that explains why your characters are the way they are, or why they behave in the way that they do.

- Go to three disparate places and spend at least half an hour there, just looking. Write down everything you see, from dust motes in the air to the colors on the wall to scars on the surface of a tabletop. What do you smell there? Hear? Touch? Taste?

- Now describe the environment of four people, one who lives on a ranch in Texas, one who lives in a Cape Cod cottage, one who's an expat in Paris, and one who lives on a colony on the moon. Write the answer to these questions for each of the four people: What might their plans for the evening be? What drew them to where they are? If they were born there, what keeps them there?

Dialogue

Nothing can take a reader out of a story faster than dialogue that doesn't feel real. But when it's done right, dialogue can really add to or even make a story. When you're writing dialogue for characters, try as much as possible to *be* them. Make sure that your dialogue defines your characters, and that what one character says isn't interchangeable with what another one does.

And always, in the back of your mind, keep asking this question: Do real people talk like this?

Here are some exercises that will help you listen carefully, and then help you translate what you hear into real-sounding dialogue.

- Take yourself to a place where you can sit and listen to people talk: a train station, a beauty parlor, a coffee shop. Write down exactly what you hear, including hesitations and corrections and repetitions and throat clearings, and note too the emotion that seems to be underlying what is said. It can be especially interesting to write someone saying one thing while obviously feeling another.

- At home, without looking at your notes, try to re-create the conversations you overheard. Use lines of dialogue only, no description, no "he said," "she said." Add at least two or three things of your own, things that weren't said, things that you just make up and that you insert between lines of dialogue you overheard. For example, perhaps you heard someone say, "I doubt that will happen." You can change it to "Yeah, like that would ever happen." Or you can add on, "I doubt that will happen. At least not in our lifetimes, or our children's. Or their children's."

- Now, using the real people you eavesdropped on, make up a conversation of your own to give them. For example, what might the people have said after you left? How would each of them describe the conversation they had to another person when they got home?

- Imagine a fight between two significant others. Make up your own or use this one: A came home late without calling B to let him/her know. Write out the fight, using lines of dialogue only.

- Now imagine that same fight in different locations: at a ball park, in a church, at a relative's house for Sunday dinner, at ▶

a deserted waterfront, in the couple's bedroom. Keep the same basic fight, but now set the scene and add details about the environment the couple is in. Also, make some changes in the dialogue that accommodate or reflect that environment.

Macro and Micro

Here's an exercise that will help show you that the macro can always be in the micro, and vice versa.

- Consider a common object: A necklace. A carton of milk. A shoe. A front porch. Then write a scene where your character is using that object in an ordinary way. Now enlarge the scene by having your character make some connection to something much bigger, inspired by that object.

- Now let's go in the other direction. Put a character in a dramatic situation: A war. A flood. An incredible journey. Now have that character change focus. Have him, for example, find something in his pocket that means something to him. In the midst of chaos, have him concentrate on that one small thing.

Using First Lines as Springboards

One of the stories I wrote that I like best was inspired by my having been given a first line by someone else. Something about it coming from nowhere freed me up. Try this exercise and see what you come up with.

- Use these first lines to send you off on a creative journey. The key here is not to think too much; just use whatever pops into your head to write the next sentence. Write one sentence only, or, if you become inspired, keep going. You may end up with your own story.

  – *After the rain stopped, I went out.*
  – *The last time he called me, I hung up on him.*
  – *Annie puts whipped cream on everything.*

– If I were to design a waiting room, it wouldn't look like this.
– The first time I drove all night, I was seventeen

- Now make up five first sentences of your own. And then write five sentences you think would make good last sentences. ◠

A Few Thoughts About Reading and Inspiration

I RECOMMEND BOOKS ALL THE TIME, in print and otherwise. But I believe in people finding their own treasures, their own inspiration—and for reasons of their own. That's really the spirit of *Escaping into the Open*, to be true to who you are as an individual. Too often I find people slogging through *this* when what they need is *that*.

There are a number of books that I turn to again and again for pleasure and encouragement. Every time I do a reading, I recommend anything by Alice Munro, the short stories of Michael Byers, the novels of Anne Tyler and Elizabeth Strout and Mark Slouka, essays by E. B. White, and poetry by Billy Collins and Jane Hirshfield. I love the graphic novels of Art Spiegelman and the comics of Lynda Barry. Those make up *my* go-to reading list.

Yours will be different, and I urge you to look for it. Make time to wander the stacks in bookstores and libraries to see what jumps into your hands. ✺